Diving & Snorkeling

British Virgin Islands

Mauricio Handler

LONELY PLANET PUBLICATIONS
Melbourne • Oakland • London • Paris

Diving & Snorkeling British Virgin Islands
- A Lonely Planet Pisces Book

2nd Edition – January 2001
1st Edition – 1992, Gulf Publishing Company

Published by
Lonely Planet Publications
90 Maribyrnong St., Footscray, Victoria 3011, Australia

Other offices
150 Linden Street, Oakland, California 94607, USA
10a Spring Place, London NW5 3BH, UK
1 rue du Dahomey, 75011 Paris, France

Photographs
by Mauricio Handler unless otherwise indicated

Front cover photograph, by Mauricio Handler
Divers at The Baths, Virgin Gorda

Back cover photographs, by Mauricio Handler
Blue-striped lizardfish
Cannon under bow section, RMS *Rhone*
Catamaran at The Indians

All of the images in this guide are available for
    licensing from **Lonely Planet Images**
email: lpi@lonelyplanet.com.au

ISBN 1 86450 135 9

text & maps © Lonely Planet 2001
photographs © photographers as indicated 2001
Rhone drawing © George & Luana Marler
Wreck of the RMS Rhone painting © National Maritime
Museum, London
dive site maps are Transverse Mercator projection

LONELY PLANET and the Lonely Planet logo are
trademarks of Lonely Planet Publications Pty Ltd.

Printed by H&Y Printing Ltd., Hong Kong

Contents

Diving in the British Virgin Islands 33

Northwest Dive Sites 38

Tobago Cays 40

Jost Van Dyke 45

Great Thatch Island 48

Tortola 50

Guana Island 54

Great Camanoe Island 55

Southwest Dive Sites 56

Norman Island 58

Author

Mauricio Handler

Born in Chile, Mauricio was raised in Michigan, USA and completed a bachelor's degree in fine arts at the University of Puerto Rico. He holds a U.S. Coast Guard 100-ton captain's license, which he used extensively for eight years while running a private 60ft sailing vessel throughout the Caribbean. Since 1985, Mauricio has worked as a commercial marine photo-journalist based out of the British Virgin Islands. His work has appeared in numerous publications. Mauricio also works as an underwater photography assistant for David Doubilet of *National Geographic*. When not traveling on assignment, Mauricio is busy running his commercial photography business in Tortola, where he lives with his wife Michele and twin daughters Maya and Taylor.

JOSEPH STANCAMPIANO

From the Author

I would like to thank the following people, who helped in a multitude of ways to make the research and photography for this book a pleasurable experience: Randy Keil, for his knowledge and friendship over the years. Sue Thompson, one of the most knowledgeable guides to work in the BVI: without her insight this guide would have been incomplete. Julia Leroy, my research and photography assistant, whose meticulous attention to detail kept me out of trouble many times over. Gary Cotreau and Gary Fisher for their assistance and companionship while diving. My wife Michele, for putting up with me and my dreams and my ever-changing schedule. My mother Sonia, who in 1977 reluctantly allowed me to don a scuba tank for the first time off the waters of La Parguera, Puerto Rico. My clients in the BVI, whose support over the years have allowed me to remain in the islands. Michael and Marietta Satz, who for eight years believed in me and gave the scarcest of commodities: time. I dedicate this, my first solo dive guide, to my twin daughters Maya and Taylor, whom I hope will grow up to discover and enjoy this beautiful part of the world, and to explore the underwater life that anxiously awaits them.

Photography Notes

Mauricio uses Nikon cameras and lenses exclusively, except in certain situations where a housed Mamiya 6x7 format camera is required. He drags along Nikon F3s, an N90 and, recently, a Nikon F100. Mauricio uses a wide selection of lenses, from the ultra-wide 16mm to the 105 macro. Although most of the lenses are auto-focus, he continues to make images in the manual mode. Recently, Mauricio has begun to use TTL for selected detailed macro work. He uses Ikeleite strobes: 150s, 200s and some slave MS units. All strobes are connected to the housings using TLC arms. Cameras are housed in Aquatica Housings by Aqua Vision in Montreal, Canada. Mauricio exposes the hundreds of rolls of film throughout the year; he uses Fuji Velvia (50 asa), Provia 100F and Kodak Ektachrome 100VS when he needs an additional stop. For black and white, he uses Kodak Tri-X 400 and 3200.

The majority of the photos in this book were provided by Mauricio Handler. Additional images were provided by Steve Simonsen, Steve Rosenberg, Len Zell and Michael McKay.

From the Publisher

This second edition was produced in Lonely Planet's U.S. office under direction from Roslyn Bullas, the Pisces Books publishing manager. Wendy Smith edited the book, with many invaluable editorial contributions from fellow editor David Lauterborn. David also performed copious additional research and wrote a number of the sidebars. Eagle-eyed proofreader Wendy Taylor helped clean up our act in the final moments. Ruth Askevold designed the book's contents, which were finalized by Emily Douglas, who also created the cover. John Spelman, Sara Nelson, Annette Olson and Kat Smith created the maps, which were adapted from the author's base maps, under the supervision of U.S. Cartography Manager Alex Guilbert. Justin Marler produced the *Rhone* wreck illustration, which was originally created by George Marler (no relation) and adapted by David Lauterborn. The photograph of William Frederick Mitchell's painting *Wreck of the RMS Rhone* appears courtesy of the National Maritime Museum in London.

Pisces Pre-Dive Safety Guidelines

Before embarking on a scuba diving, skin diving or snorkeling trip, carefully consider the following to help ensure a safe and enjoyable experience:

- Possess a current diving certification card from a recognized scuba diving instructional agency (if scuba diving)
- Be sure you are healthy and feel comfortable diving
- Obtain reliable information about physical and environmental conditions at the dive site (e.g., from a reputable local dive operation)
- Be aware of local laws, regulations and etiquette about marine life and environment
- Dive at sites within your experience level; if possible, engage the services of a competent, professionally trained dive instructor or divemaster

Underwater conditions vary significantly from one region, or even site, to another. Seasonal changes can significantly alter site and dive conditions. These differences influence the way divers dress for a dive and what diving techniques they use.

There are special requirements for diving in any area, regardless of location. Before your dive, ask about environmental characteristics that can affect your diving and how trained local divers deal with these considerations.

Warning & Request

Things change—dive site conditions, regulations, topside information. Nothing stays the same for long. Your feedback on this book will be used to help update and improve the next edition. Excerpts from your correspondence may appear in *Planet Talk*, our quarterly newsletter, or *Comet*, our monthly email newsletter. Please let us know if you do not want your letter published or your name acknowledged.

Correspondence can be addressed to:
Lonely Planet Publications
Pisces Books
150 Linden Street
Oakland, CA 94607
email: pisces@lonelyplanet.com

Introduction

Less developed and less known internationally than many of their Caribbean neighbors, the British Virgin Islands (BVI) have managed to remain relatively unspoiled. The lack of direct international flights into the territory, in addition to concerted efforts to curb large-scale tourist development, make the islands a getaway vacation area known principally to sailors and divers.

For the yachting crowd, the BVI is prized for its constant easterly trade winds and its many protected anchorages. Perhaps the best way to get to know the territory is to sail between the principal ports, stopping to explore myriad sandy islands, small islets and rocky outcrops. These largely uninhabited, secluded islands bear evocative names—including the Dogs, Green Cay, Sandy Spit, Fallen Jerusalem, the Indians and Dead Chest—that reveal a place rich in pirate and seafaring lore. Yacht charters of all shapes and sizes are available to the experienced boat handler, while day charters and crewed yachts allow less-seaworthy visitors to get in on the action.

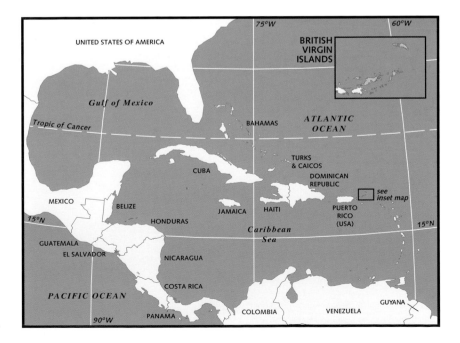

In the BVI, diving and boating go hand in hand. With few exceptions, diving is done from boats rather than from shore. Conditions are pleasant—average water temperatures are warm, and currents and weather rarely pose much of a problem at the more popular spots, so diving is a year-round affair.

Dive sites are scattered throughout the territory, with no particular area commanding the best spots. Though there are many beautiful, healthy reefs for divers to explore, the historic *Rhone* wreck is the most famous of all BVI sites. The mighty vessel met her fate during the Hurricane of 1867, and despite nearly a century and a half underwater, she retains an astounding number of her original features. Most divers will want to go under several times to explore the vessel's separate sections and copious coral growth. Other dive sites feature a variety of geological formations, which attract large numbers of common and rare Caribbean fish and invertebrate species.

The 63 dive sites covered in this book represent a range of the best and most popular sites around the British Virgin Islands. The sites are divided into five diving regions, starting with northwestern sites—which include sites near Tortola and its nearby islands—and moving counterclockwise through the territory, ending with the remote challenges around Anegada. Information about location, depth range, access and expertise level is provided for each site. You'll also find detailed descriptions of each site, noting conditions, underwater topography and the marine life you can expect to see. The Marine Life section provides a gallery of the BVI's common fish and invertebrate life. Though this book is not intended to be a stand-alone travel guide, the Practicalities and Overview sections offer useful information about the islands, while the Activities & Attractions section provides ideas about how to spend your time out of the water.

In the BVI, half the fun lies underwater—daytripping snorkelers set out for adventure.

Overview

The British Virgin Islands lie 50 miles (80km) east of Puerto Rico, 1,100 miles (1,770km) southeast of Miami and just east and north of the U.S. Virgin Islands. Tortola, Virgin Gorda, Anegada and Jost Van Dyke are the principal islands; most of the other 40-odd islets are uninhabited. Three-quarters of the BVI's population lives on Tortola, which is 12 miles (19km) long and 3 miles (5km) wide.

History

Arawak Indians settled the Virgin Islands around 100 BC, migrating up through the Lesser Antilles from the Orinoco River basin in South America. A peaceloving tribe, they were driven out by the more aggressive Caribs, who arrived from South America in the mid-15th century. Little or no trace remains of the islands' original Indian population.

Just a few decades later, in 1493, Christopher Columbus stopped by on his second trip to the New World. Columbus named the area's island group Las Vírgenes in a reference to St. Ursula and her 11,000 virgins. He also gave Virgin Gorda (Fat Virgin) and Anegada (Sunken Island) the names that remain today.

The Spanish didn't take much interest in the islands. European would-be settlers were harassed by Caribs and by pirates, who attacked galleons carrying riches back to Spain. An assortment of colorful characters sailed through the surrounding waters, including pirates Sir Henry Morgan and Edward Teach, known as Blackbeard. English privateer Sir Francis Drake sailed many times through the channel that runs between the territory's northern and southern islands—today it bears his name. The pirates and other seafarers left behind legends and treasures, some of which have not yet been discovered.

As Spain declined as a colonial power, ownership of the islands shifted about until the Dutch established a permanent settlement on Tortola in 1648. The English ousted the Dutch from Tortola in 1672 and from Anegada and Virgin Gorda in 1680. The new rulers introduced the two quintessential features of the colonial era in the Caribbean: sugarcane and slavery. By the 1700s a plantation society had been firmly established. Between the mid-18th and early 19th centuries the islands prospered, producing sugar, cotton, rum, indigo and spices.

Slave unrest and ideological doubt brought an end to slave auctions in 1803. By the 1830s, slaves had been emancipated (much earlier than in the United States). Abolition and other economic changes drove many of the white settlers to other shores—today's population is mostly descended from slaves. African influences are evident in the food, in the music and in the handmade sloops that many locals use for fishing. Islanders reflect a mixture of British and West Indian influences when playing their dashing style of cricket and when they wash down a plate of conch fritters with a pint of ale.

In 1917 the United States purchased the adjacent Danish West Indies (U.S. Virgin Islands) as a strategic outpost in the Caribbean. In the 1930s and '40s, livestock, vegetables and fishing were still the mainstay of the BVI economy, but by the 1960s, Laurance Rockefeller had leased land in Virgin Gorda and built a luxury resort at Little Dix Bay. The airport at Beef Island was opened in 1968, and the opening of the first charter yacht operator in 1969 marked the beginning of the islands' yachting industry.

To this day, the islands remain a protected territory of the British Crown, operating under direct British rule through appointed representatives and elected officials. Economically, however, the BVI is closely tied with the neighboring U.S. Virgin Islands and, by extension, the United States.

The economic and political stability of the BVI, coupled with an ideal climate and unspoiled natural surroundings, attract around 300,000 visitors a year. Local citizens have learned from the mistakes of other Caribbean islands and taken steps to guide growth, resulting in a relatively well-protected environment. Because of a relatively strict employment scheme for nonlocals (anyone not born here), which includes annual reviews of work and trade licenses, the local community boasts virtually no unemployment. The islands' burgeoning offshore banking industry may give the BVI the option of further limiting tourist growth, should they wish to.

Geography

The Virgin Islands group includes approximately 90 islands, islets and cays northeast of Puerto Rico. The BVI comprises the northeasternmost islands of the group. The Virgin Islands divide the North Atlantic from the Caribbean Sea. They are considered the easternmost of the Greater Antilles and are separated from the Lesser Antilles island chain (to the east) by the Anegada Channel.

All but one of the British Virgin Islands are of volcanic origin—the islands themselves are the peaks of a submerged mountain chain. Anegada, 15 miles (24km) north of Tortola, is the only island of coral origin in the group. The prized white sandy beaches tend to occupy the

Some of Guana Island's native flamingos.

north and west coasts of the islands, while the southern shores are usually rocky. Dense tropical forests cover most of the islands' inland hills, but there are also arid stretches dominated by succulents, palms and coastal mangrove swamps, where crabs scuttle about and juvenile fish find their swimming fins.

Indigenous forest fauna includes mahogany, bulletwood, fig, tree ferns and the elephant-ear vine, which slithers along the ground until it finds a sturdy tree to climb. Mango, papaya, coconut and breadfruit trees are found in abundance. Common animals are lizards, rats, donkeys, goats and mongooses. The nocturnal bo-peep frog is found exclusively on Virgin Gorda and Tortola and has a call that seems impossibly loud for such a little critter. Virgin Gorda is home to a tiny gecko with the distinction of having a name (*Spherodactylus pathenopian*) longer than the animal itself. Birds include doves, hummingbirds, herons, egrets and hawks.

The islands rise from a relatively shallow undersea plateau and are surrounded by fringing reefs. There are no steep drop-offs close to shore, though divers will find shallow walls less than 100ft (30m) deep. The area's volcanic origins are evident at the many sites that feature pinnacles, caves, ledges and swim-throughs, accompanied by high-rising corals. For divers, the coral island of Anegada is characterized by shipwrecks—nautical casualties of the vast shallow reef that extends southeast of the island.

Chip off the Old Reef

Primarily volcanic in origin, the Virgin Islands are a geological extension of Puerto Rico's central mountains and lie along the same fault line. The islands are hilly and ecologically similar—except for Anegeda.

Anegada—whose Spanish name translates as "inundated" or "sunken"—is a low-lying coral reef island. In fact, at 28ft (8.4m), its highest point isn't even visible to approaching boats until they are literally upon the surrounding reef—a trait that has lured hundreds of ships to their watery graves.

Horseshoe Reef is a large crescent-shaped reef that extends 11 miles (18km) southeast of the island. It is the third-largest reef in the world (after the barrier reef systems of Australia and Belize) and actually spawned the island it protects. Through the ages, waves and storm action broke off bits of coral from the reef, which mixed with finer particles to form reeftop shoals. Rainwater dissolved exposed coral skeletons into lime, which fused with the sand to form the landmass. Beaches developed, and the island was gradually colonized by hardy plants and animals, which contribute their own waste and remains to the island, helping soil develop. The island of Anegada, therefore, is really a smaller, newer part of its sprawling coral parent.

British Virgin Islands

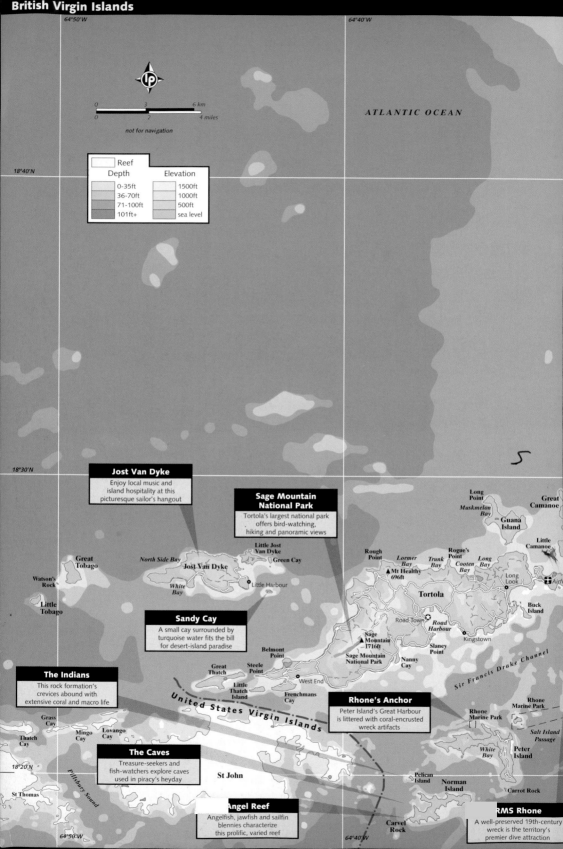

64°50'W   64°40'W

ATLANTIC OCEAN

0   3   6 km
0   2   4 miles

not for navigation

Reef	
Depth	**Elevation**
0-35ft	1500ft
36-70ft	1000ft
71-100ft	500ft
101ft+	sea level

18°40'N

18°30'N

Jost Van Dyke
Enjoy local music and island hospitality at this picturesque sailor's hangout

Sage Mountain National Park
Tortola's largest national park offers bird-watching, hiking and panoramic views

Sandy Cay
A small cay surrounded by turquoise water fits the bill for desert-island paradise

The Indians
This rock formation's crevices abound with extensive coral and macro life

The Caves
Treasure-seekers and fish-watchers explore caves used in piracy's heyday

Rhone's Anchor
Peter Island's Great Harbour is littered with coral-encrusted wreck artifacts

Angel Reef
Angelfish, jawfish and sailfin blennies characterize this prolific, varied reef

RMS Rhone
A well-preserved 19th-century wreck is the territory's premier dive attraction

Long Point
Great Camanoe
Muskmelon Bay
Guana Island
Little Camanoe
Rough Point
Lormer Bay
Trunk Bay
Rogue's Point
Cooten Bay
Long Bay
Long Look
▲ Mt Healthy 696ft
Tortola
Road Town
Road Harbour
Kingstown
Buck Island
▲ Sage Mountain 1716ft
Sage Mountain National Park
Slaney Point
Nanny Cay
Sir Francis Drake Channel

Little Jost Van Dyke
Green Cay
Great Tobago
North Side Bay
Jost Van Dyke
White Bay
Little Harbour
Watson's Rock
Little Tobago

Belmont Point
Great Thatch
Steele Point
Little Thatch Island
Frenchmans Cay
West End

United States Virgin Islands

Grass Cay
Mingo Cay
Lovango Cay
Thatch Cay
St Thomas
Pillsbury Sound

St John

Rhone Marine Park
Rhone Marine Park
Salt Island Passage
White Bay
Peter Island

Pelican Island
Norman Island
Carrot Rock

Carvel Rock

18°20'N

64°50'W   64°40'W

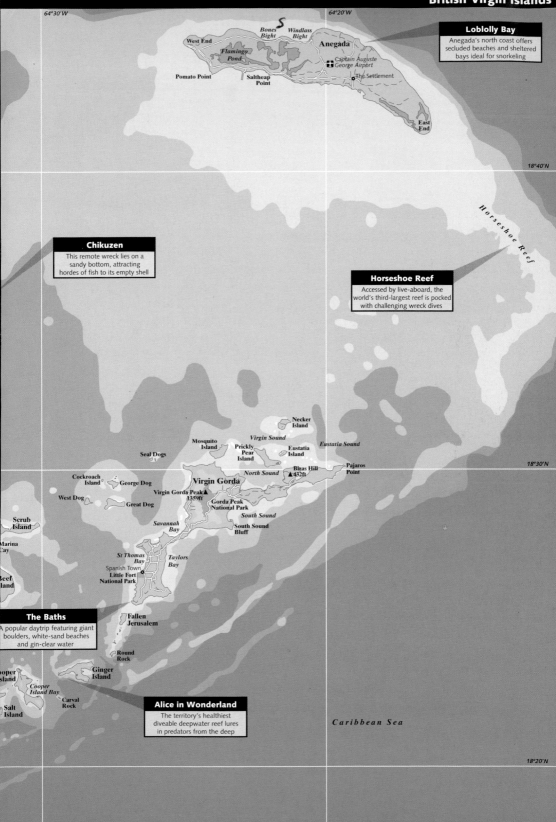

Loblolly Bay
Anegada's north coast offers secluded beaches and sheltered bays ideal for snorkeling

West End
Bones Bight
Windlass Bight
Anegada
Flamingo Pond
Captain Auguste George Airport
Pomato Point
Saltheap Point
The Settlement
East End

Horseshoe Reef

Chikuzen
This remote wreck lies on a sandy bottom, attracting hordes of fish to its empty shell

Horseshoe Reef
Accessed by live-aboard, the world's third-largest reef is pocked with challenging wreck dives

Necker Island
Virgin Sound
Mosquito Island
Prickly Pear Island
Eustatia Island
Eustatia Sound
Seal Dogs
Biras Hill ▲432ft
Pajaros Point
Cockroach Island
George Dog
Virgin Gorda
North Sound
West Dog
Virgin Gorda Peak▲ 1359ft
Great Dog
Gorda Peak National Park
South Sound
Scrub Island
Savannah Bay
South Sound Bluff
Marina Cay
St Thomas Bay
Taylors Bay
eef land
Spanish Town
Little Fort National Park

The Baths
A popular daytrip featuring giant boulders, white-sand beaches and gin-clear water

Fallen Jerusalem
ooper Island
Round Rock
Cooper Island Bay
Ginger Island
Carval Rock
Salt Island

Alice in Wonderland
The territory's healthiest diveable deepwater reef lures in predators from the deep

Caribbean Sea

64°30'W
64°20'W
18°40'N
18°30'N
18°20'N

Practicalities

Climate

The BVI is blessed with favorable weather year-round. Temperatures range between a low of about 65°F (18°C) during winter nights to about 90°F (32°C) during summer days. August and September are the hottest months of the year—if you're sailing through, however, you may not feel the heat as much as those who are land-based.

Water temperatures range between about 78° and 84°F (26° and 29°C). Sea conditions within the Sir Francis Drake Channel vary throughout the year, ranging from flat, glassy waters to 10ft (3m) hurricane waves. Average conditions, however, are relatively comfortable for diving, with a 3ft (1m) or less chop.

The territory is dry—average annual rainfall is about 38 inches (97cm) per year. Though residents complain that it doesn't rain enough, visitors rarely see poor weather. Rain is more likely during hurricane season (July through October). Hurricane season should not deter anyone from visiting, as it is during this time that diving conditions are optimal. Calm seas and gentle breezes open up many sites that are inaccessible during the winter.

Winds blow year-round, with the strongest winds during the winter from November to April. The strong, steady easterly trade winds make this area arguably the world's most popular sailing destination.

A Note on Hurricane Season

Hurricane season in the Caribbean and North Atlantic officially begins on June 1 and runs until November 1. You can expect at least one of these fierce cyclonic storms to pass near or through the territory at some point during the season—hopefully not during your vacation!

Most hurricanes will cause little or no damage as they pass through. In a larger-than-normal storm, be sure to follow any and all evacuation or other safety instructions. Because of the potential damage of a killer storm, it is wise to carry travel insurance, especially if you are chartering a yacht.

Meteorologists now provide excellent forecasting during hurricane season, so you'll usually have four or five days warning before a storm rolls through. For daily forecasts, contact Tortola's Caribbean Weather Center (☎ 496-9000) or visit its website at www.caribwx.com.

Language

English is the official language of the BVI. That said, locals pepper their speech with a range of colorful West Indian expressions and accents.

Getting There

There are no direct flights to the BVI from the U.S., Canada or Europe. Connecting flights are available through San Juan, Puerto Rico or, less frequently, through St. Thomas in the U.S. Virgin Islands. Flights arrive at the international airport on Beef Island, which is connected to Tortola's east coast by a short bridge. There is a small airport on Virgin Gorda and an airstrip on Anegada. Ferries shuttle between the main ports of both the British and the U.S. Virgin Islands.

The BVI is a popular stopover for cruise ships—the mammoth boats arrive daily in the busy winter season (November to May). The cruise ship dock in Road Town is the primary port of call.

Visitors cross this small bridge to get from the airport on Beef Island to the Tortola mainland.

Gateway City – Road Town

Road Town, the territory's small capital, lies on Tortola's southern shore. On Waterfront Drive—the main civic street, which runs along the shore—you'll find the Governor's House, the main hospital and other businesses. Parallel to Waterfront Drive you'll find Main Street, the only part of the island that retains some of the old West Indian architecture and charm. It is a narrow street full of shops, boutiques and specialty stores and is also the site of several historical buildings, such as the old prison. The ferry terminal—which also houses customs and immigration offices—is across from the main plaza in the center of town.

Getting Around

Though it is possible to fly between the major islands, anyone who's done it will tell you that the very best way to get around the BVI is by chartered sailboat. There are loads of crewed and bareboat (without crew) charter operators throughout the territory. You'll have to take a proficiency test before you're allowed to go it alone, and your experience level will determine the size and type of boat you're eligible to rent. Night sailing and sailing near Anegada, where waters can be treacherous, are prohibited.

A convenient and less-expensive way to island-hop in the Virgin Islands is the network of interisland ferries—reservations are not necessary, but call ahead for schedules. Another option for shorter trips is to hire a motorboat.

Red-legged tortoises explore Road Town.

Because the BVI's road system is limited, driving is a reasonable option only on the main islands. Tortola has a fine road network, and Virgin Gorda and Anegada both have several streets to get you where you need to go. There are car rental agencies on Tortola, Virgin Gorda and Anegada. You'll need a temporary local driver's license (get it when you rent the car) and a valid license from home. Driving in the BVI may take some getting used to—the cars have the steering wheel on the left (U.S. standard), but driving is on the left (British standard).

It's not hard to find a taxi on Tortola, but it's more difficult on the other islands. Rates are fixed and based on the distance and number of passengers. If you bring your own bicycle to the islands, you're supposed to register it with the traffic office in Road Town.

Entry

All visitors to the BVI—except citizens of the U.S. and Canada—will need a valid passport. U.S. and Canadian citizens will need proof of citizenship (a birth certificate or voter registration card will do) and a valid ID. Some foreign visitors need visas. Others, including citizens of the British Commonwealth and its

The pace of life in the islands provides plenty of opportunities for reflective relaxation.

dependent territories, do not need visas to enter. For detailed information about visa requirements, contact the BVI Immigration Office (☎ 494-2538).

Time

The BVI is on Atlantic Standard Time, one hour ahead of Eastern Standard Time and four hours behind GMT. When it's noon in the BVI, it's 11am in New York, 4pm in London, 8am in San Francisco and 1am the following morning in Sydney. Daylight saving time is not observed.

Money

The BVI's official currency is the U.S. dollar. Not all BVI banks carry international currency exchange services, so it's best to arrive with U.S. dollars. Cash advances on credit cards (MasterCard or Visa) are available. Major credit cards are widely accepted, though businesses on some of the smaller islands may prefer cash. Traveler's checks are accepted with a photo ID and a contact number within the islands. A 10% to 15% gratuity is added to most restaurant bills. A 7% government tax and a 10% service charge are added to all hotel bills.

Electricity

As in the U.S., voltage in the BVI is 110 volts/60 cycles, and plugs have two flat pins or three pins (two flat, one round). Plugs with three pins don't fit into a two-hole socket, but adapters are easy to find at hardware stores. Virtually all live-aboards follow these standards, but it's wise to call to confirm.

Weights & Measures

The BVI uses the imperial system. Distance is measured in miles, temperature in degrees Fahrenheit, length in feet and inches, and weight in pounds and ounces. This book provides both imperial and metric measurements, except for specific references within dive site descriptions, which are given in imperial units only. For reference, use the conversion chart inside the back cover of this book.

What to Bring

Casual dress is the norm. Unless you are lodging or dining in the evening at one of the BVI's top resorts, you won't need formal attire. If you're staying on a live-aboard, you may need a light sweater or long-sleeved shirt. A waterproof jacket is useful for unexpected showers and for after-diving chills. Beach goods—sunscreen, towels and clothing—are readily available. There are well-stocked pharmacies, but it is always wise to fill prescriptions before leaving home.

Avid divers will usually bring their own BC, regulator, mask, snorkel, fins, wetsuit and diving computer. All equipment is readily available for rent. Equipment sales are limited.

Water temperatures in the BVI are warm, but a 3mm full wetsuit is advisable for extended diving and as protection against coral. In the winter, you may wish to use a heavier suit.

Underwater Photography

Photographers and videographers with the usual load of paraphernalia and variations in technical equipment should be sure to carry spare equipment for emergencies. A good selection of camera batteries is available locally, but if you require a specific type, you should bring extras. Be sure that all rechargeable batteries and packs are 110 volts/60 cycles, or bring an adapter.

Videotape of all formats, including 8mm, Hi8, mini-DV (digital) and VHS, are relatively easy to find, but only for the NTSC system, which is standard in the U.S. If you are running the PAL system, bring your own.

Business Hours

Regular business hours are weekdays 9am to 5pm. Banks are usually open weekdays 9am to 3pm. Most shops are open weekdays 9am to 5pm and Saturday 9am to 1pm.

Accommodations

Accommodations in the BVI range from campgrounds to luxury resorts. A handful of resort hotels cater specifically to the dive traveler, with operators on the premises. Most BVI dive operators will care for your gear, so you won't necessarily need a wet locker or drying area in your room. There are plenty of smaller resorts, hotels and inns throughout the islands. These properties can be a bit farther away from boat docks, so you may need to rent a car. Other lodging options include self-catering villa or apartment rentals—these are usually rented by the week.

Many visitors charter a yacht, taking care of their transportation and accommodations in one shot. Many of the boats are provisioned. See the Listings section for charter companies, or connect with an independent yacht broker through the Tourist Board or while on-island.

Budget accommodations are few and far between in the BVI. Even camp-grounds are expensive by U.S. and European standards. That said, good deals can be found during the May-to-October off-season. Lodging prices are highest from November through April. The best prices are available in August and September, though many hotels and resorts close during the off-season.

A late-afternoon rainbow bathes an Anegada hotel in color.

Dining & Food

The BVI has a wide selection of restaurants and cafés to satisfy most appetites and budgets. Pick up the free *BVI Restaurant Guide* to help you make up your mind. For casual dining, look to mom-and-pop BBQs and fish-frys throughout the islands. Visitors should be sure to sample some local specialties. One favorite is *roti*, soft Indian bread filled with seafood, chicken, goat meat or vegetables and served hot with mango chutney and other spicy sauces. Or try the ever-popular johnnycake, a filling snack made from fried cornmeal dough.

A list of restaurants and their weekly specialties can be found in *Limin' Times*, the weekly entertainment publication. Well-stocked supermarkets will help you provision your rental kitchen, while specialty food shops do their best to cater to your sophisticated palate. Fine wines, champagnes and liquors are available at duty-free prices, and don't forget to sample some of the locally made rums.

Local band Blue Haze takes five from its busy musical calendar.

Shopping

Shops throughout the BVI carry local or Caribbean crafts. In Road Town be sure to stop by the **Crafts Alive** outdoor market near the ferry terminal. Here you will find a range of sarongs, straw hats and other clothing and locally made handicrafts such as baskets, dolls and wooden and wrought-iron ornaments.

For locally made jewelry, go to **Samarkand** on Main Street in Road Town. The owners hand-craft items from silver and gold and specialize in virgin jasper, the local semiprecious green stone. The **Caribbean Handprints** shop, also on Main Street, is known for its unique printed fabrics. You can purchase clothing or get material by the yard. Just a short walk farther up Main Street, look for **Sunny Caribee**, a unique shop that carries beautifully packaged island-made preserves, sauces and spices. Next door, their art gallery shows artwork by local and Caribbean artists. Other shops throughout the islands carry everything from local rums and spices to cigars.

Please refrain from purchasing any black-coral or turtle-shell products you may see for sale in the BVI. These products deplete fragile populations and, in the case of sea-turtle shell products, are illegal.

Activities & Attractions

Activities and attractions in the BVI generally revolve around the water—whether you're yachting, lounging on the beach, kayaking or surfing, you're likely to get wet. Even most of the topside activities, such as hiking or horseback riding, are often designed to get you somewhere with a good ocean view.

National Parks

The BVI is blessed with many natural attractions, most of which are protected as part of the National Parks Trust. You can buy a guide to the territory's national parks, with complete descriptions and photographs, from local bookstores and newsstands.

Tortola's **Sage Mountain National Park** contains the highest point on the island, reaching to 1,716ft (515m). This beautiful, densely wooded forest boasts many ferns, elephant-ear plants, fig trees and other local flora. It is also a haven for small birds, butterflies and flowers. A variety of hiking paths lead you through the park and to the summit of Sage Mountain.

The 4-acre (1.6-hectare) **J.R. O'Neal Botanical Gardens** are in Road Town, just east of the town center. The gardens abound with indigenous and exotic tropical plants. There is a fountain, an aviary and a lily pond. It is a great place to picnic or just relax.

Virgin Gorda's mountainous interior is protected as the **Gorda Peak National Park**—its highest point reaches 1,389ft (417m). Once cleared for lumber, much of the area has been reforested with mahogany trees. Bromeliads and orchids litter the easy and well-maintained trails leading to the peak. The observation tower offers wonderful panoramic views.

Yachting

Over the years, the BVI has gained a well-deserved reputation as a world-class sailing ground. Here you can learn to sail a one-person boat from the local yacht club or take to open waters on a crewed or bareboat (without crew) charter. In either case, it is an enriching way to experience the islands.

Daysails are the easiest and most economical way to get your hands on a million-dollar yacht. It is easy to charter anything for a day, from a traditional schooner to an ultramodern catamaran.

For longer trips, yacht brokers and charter companies throughout the islands can help you set sail. When arranging a bareboat charter, you'll be asked to provide a résumé of your boat-handling experience—your skill level will determine the size and type of vessel you are eligible to commandeer. Nonsailors can charter crewed boats and sit back to enjoy the ride.

If you're looking to learn to sail for the first time, contact the Royal BVI Yacht Club (☎ 494-3286) or Offshore Sailing School (toll-free ☎ 800-221-4326) in Road Town. On Virgin Gorda, try the Bitter End Yacht Club (☎ 494-2745).

New Year's Eve attracts an extra-large yachting crowd to Great Harbour, Jost Van Dyke.

Horseback Riding

Horseback riding is a great way to slow down the pace of any vacation. Trails are gentle and offer great views. For arrangements, contact Shadows Stable (☎ 494-2262) on Ridge Road in Tortola or Alex Parillon (☎ 495-5110) on Virgin Gorda.

Museums & Tours

Most people don't come to the BVI to poke around in museums, but while you're here, there are a few spots of historic and cultural interest worth checking out.

On Road Town's Main Street, the **Virgin Islands Folk Museum** displays artifacts from the wreck of the *Rhone* and from the plantation era, including china, silverware and bottles. On Tortola's east end, the **Josiah's Bay Plantation Art Gallery** is housed in a former rum distillery. In addition to the gallery and gift shop that can be perused, distillery relics are on display. For those especially interested in the local spirits, the **Callwood Rum Distillery** in Cane Garden Bay still produces rum in much the same way it did 200 years ago. The building is from the plantation era. Bring your own bottle to fill!

On the southwest tip of Virgin Gorda, you can explore the ruins of an old **copper mine** used by Cornish miners between 1838 and 1867. Today, the chimney, boiler house, cistern and mine shafts remain preserved.

Summer Fest

The BVI Summer Fest— held each year at the beginning of August—is a two-week-long riot of noise and color. Calypso, fungi and steel-pan bands shake it up, pageants crown festival queens and people flood the streets. The festival is the BVI's own version of Carnival and celebrates the emancipation of the islands' African slaves. Most of the activity takes place in Road Town.

Watersports

Diving and snorkeling aren't the only way to get wet in the BVI. Because of the constant breezes, **windsurfing** is a year-round activity. The BVI even hosts a world-class windsurfing event—the week-long HIHO (Hook In and Hold On) Race. For the average recreational windsurfer, a rental from Last Stop Sports (☎ 494-0564), HIHO (☎ 494-7694) or Windsurfing BVI (☎ 495-2447) will do the trick.

Looking out at Virgin Gorda's famed snorkeling site, The Baths.

Kayaking is gaining more popularity in the islands. The territory's many calm bays offer kayakers an up-close view of the pristine coastline. Last Stop Sports, HIHO, and Windsurfing BVI offer excursions and rental equipment.

During the winter, swells build up along north coast beaches, offering good surfing possibilities. Tortola's Little Apple Bay is the primary local favorite. If it's really rolling in, Cane Garden Bay can be excellent.

For an unusual treat, try a daysail aboard the Gli Gli Canoe (☎ 495-1849), a traditional Arawak dugout sailing canoe based out of Tortola's Trellis Bay.

Mountain Biking

Mountain biking is one of the fastest-growing sports in the islands. Tortola's cycling club was established in 1994 and today boasts some 40 members. The

The BVI offers steep hills and flats that will satisfy bikers of all skill levels.

cycling club sponsors nearly a dozen bike races each year, including one on Virgin Gorda and one on Anegada. Bike rentals are available from Last Stop Sports (☎ 494-0564).

Nightlife

If you're not going underwater at night, you'll find an assortment of activities around the islands to entertain you. The best source for up-to-date events information is *Limin' Times*, the local entertainment weekly.

Nights on the main islands can be spent dancing to the Caribbean rhythms of steel-pan bands, reggae, soca, calypso and fungi, as well as the occasional jazz, rock or blues. All dress is casual. Most places offer a happy hour, usually 5 to 7pm, when drinks are half price.

Each Thursday is nickel-beer night at Pusser's, a Tortola favorite—drink all night for the change in your pocket. On Norman Island you can indulge at the *Willy T*, the territory's only floating bar. The *Willy T*—short for William Thornton, a signer of the U.S. Declaration of Independence who was born on Little Jost Van Dyke—has a short-order restaurant, good drinks and lots of spontaneous parties. Transportation from Tortola is available. Other bars and restaurants serve up good times around the outer islands. Popular spots include Foxy's on Jost Van Dyke and the Cooper Island Beach Bar.

Each month on the night of the full moon, Bomba's sponsors one of the wildest parties in the territory. Bomba's is a shack built right on the beach at Apple Bay on Tortola's north shore. The party features live music, international crowds and general bad behavior.

Diving Health & Safety

The BVI is a generally healthy destination and poses no serious health risks to most visitors. One concern is dengue fever, a mosquito-borne disease that produces sudden high fever, muscle and joint pain and a rash, which generally subside after a few days. Though the disease itself is untreatable, hospitals can treat the symptoms if necessary. The best way to deal with dengue is to avoid it by using mosquito repellents liberally. The tropical sun is probably the most substantial concern for the average visitor—any daytime outdoor activity can lead to sunburn, and the heat (especially when combined with alcohol consumption) can cause dehydration. Divers should cover up and/or wear sunscreen and drink plenty of water.

The U.S. Centers for Disease Control & Prevention regularly posts updates on health-related concerns around the world specifically for travelers. Contact the CDC by fax or visit the website. Call (toll-free from the U.S.) ☎ 888-232-3299 and request Document 000005 to receive a list of information sheets available by fax. The website is www.cdc.gov.

Pre-Trip Preparation

Your general state of health, diving skill level and specific equipment needs are the three most important factors that impact any dive trip. If you honestly assess these before you leave, you'll be well on your way to assuring a safe dive trip.

First, if you're not in shape, start exercising. Second, if you haven't dived for a while (six months is too long) and your skills are rusty, do a local dive with an experienced buddy or take a scuba review course. Finally, inspect your dive gear. Feeling good physically, diving with experience and with reliable equipment will not only increase your safety, but will also enhance your enjoyment underwater.

At least a month before your trip, inspect your dive gear. Remember, your regulator should be serviced annually, whether you've used it or not. If you use a dive computer and can replace the battery yourself, change it before the trip or buy a spare one to take along. Otherwise, send the computer to the manufacturer for battery replacement.

If possible, find out if the dive center rents or services the type of gear you own. If not, you might want to take spare parts or even spare gear. A spare mask is always a good idea.

Purchase any additional equipment you might need, such as a dive light and tank marker light for night diving, a line reel for wreck diving, etc. Make sure you have at least a whistle attached to your BC. Better yet, add a marker tube (also known as a safety sausage or come-to-me).

About a week before taking off, do a final check of your gear, grease o-rings, check batteries and assemble a save-a-dive kit. This kit should at minimum contain extra mask and fin straps, snorkel keeper, mouthpiece, valve cap, zip ties and o-rings. Don't forget to pack a first-aid kit and medications such as decongestants, ear drops, antihistamines and seasickness tablets.

Diving & Flying

Many divers in the British Virgin Islands arrive by plane. While under most circumstances it's fine to dive soon *after* flying, it's important to remember that your last dive should be completed at least 12 hours (some experts advise 24 hours, particularly after repetitive dives) *before* your flight to minimize risk of decompression sickness, caused by residual nitrogen in the blood.

Tips for Evaluating a Dive Operator

BVI dive boats can be anything from a small boat to an elegant live-aboard. Before departure, take a good look at the craft you will be diving from. A well-outfitted dive boat has communication with onshore services. It also carries oxygen, a recall device and a first-aid kit. A well-prepared crew will give a thorough pre-dive briefing that explains procedures for dealing with an emergency

Hip and stylish mesh nets spruce up your drab dive tanks.

when divers are in the water. The briefing also explains how divers should enter the water and get back onboard. A larger boat should have a shaded area and a supply of fresh drinking water.

If there is a strong current, the crew might provide a special descent line and should be able to throw out a drift line from the stern. For deep dives the crew should hang a safety tank at 15ft (5m). On night dives a good boat will have powerful lights, including a strobe light.

When carrying groups, a good crew will get everyone's name on the dive roster so that it can initiate an immediate search if a diver is missing. This is something you should always verify.

These basic guidelines also apply to yachts that offer diving as part of their sailing itinerary. BVI dive operators are very professional and have the highest standards. The competitive nature of the business and the expense of doing business in the territory weed out sloppy operations and boats. Nevertheless, it is wise to judge for yourself and know what to look for.

Medical & Recompression Facilities

Though standards of medical services are adequate in the BVI, the territory's sleepy nature means that care can be difficult to access. For this reason, it is important that your dive boat carries adequate first-aid supplies (including oxygen) and has an established emergency procedure. In a diving emergency, call **VISAR** on radio Channel 16.

There are no recompression facilities in the BVI. The nearest recompression chamber is in St. Thomas, U.S. Virgin Islands, but the facility is considered by some to be unreliable. Other nearby chambers are on Puerto Rico and Saba. In the event of a diving emergency, contact DAN or VISAR for immediate evacuation.

Peebles Hospital
Road Town
☎ 494-3497
Emergency care

Eureka Medical Clinic
Road Town
☎ 494-2346
Family and specialist care

B&F Medical Complex
Road Town and East End
☎ 494-2196
Family and specialist care

The Bougainvillea Clinic
Road Town
☎ 494-2181
Emergency care for burns, lacerations and hand injuries

DAN

Divers Alert Network (DAN) is an international membership association of individuals and organizations sharing a common interest in diving and safety. It operates a 24-hour diving emergency hotline in the U.S.: ☎ **919-684-8111 or 919-684-4DAN** (-4326). The latter accepts collect calls in a dive emergency. Though DAN does not directly provide medical care, it does provide advice on early treatment, evacuation and hyperbaric treatment of diving-related injuries. Divers should contact DAN for assistance as soon as a diving emergency is suspected.

DAN membership is reasonably priced and includes DAN TravelAssist, a membership benefit that covers medical air evacuation from anywhere in the world for any illness or injury. For a small additional fee, divers can get secondary insurance coverage for decompression illness. For membership questions, contact DAN at ☎ 800-446-2671 in the U.S. or ☎ 919-684-2948 elsewhere. DAN can also be reached at www.diversalertnetwork.org.

MICHAEL MCKAY

A safety sausage makes you easier to find if you get separated from the group.

VISAR

Virgin Island Search & Rescue (VISAR; ☎ 494-4357 or use radio channel 16) is the BVI's most efficient emergency rescue and evacuation service. Established in 1988, it is staffed by 50 volunteers trained in search and rescue and emergency air evacuation. VISAR monitors radio channel 16 around the clock.

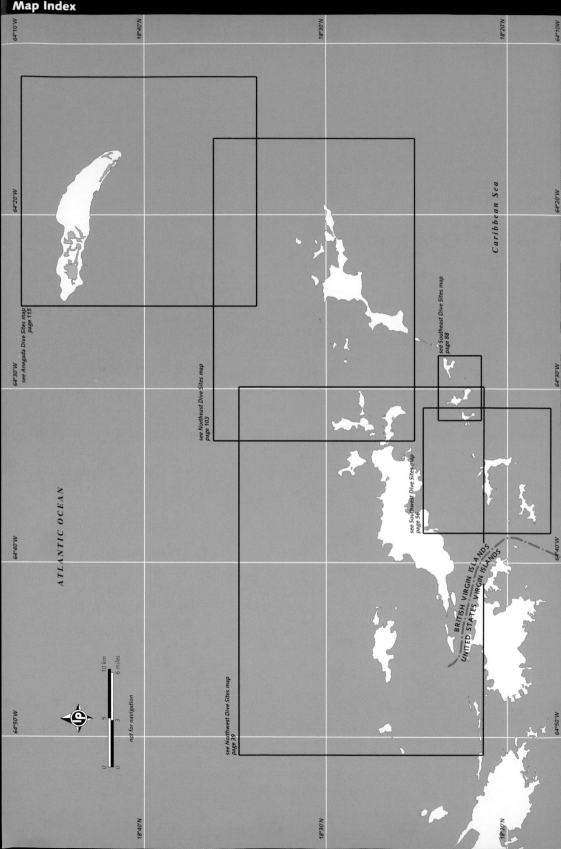

ATLANTIC OCEAN

Caribbean Sea

see Anegada Dive Sites map
page 115

see Northeast Dive Sites map
page 103

see Southeast Dive Sites map
page 88

see Southwest Dive Sites map
page 56

see Northwest Dive Sites map
page 39

BRITISH VIRGIN ISLANDS
UNITED STATES VIRGIN ISLANDS

10 km
6 miles

not for navigation

64°10'W
18°40'N
64°20'W
18°30'N
64°30'W
18°20'N
64°40'W
64°50'W
64°10'W
18°40'N
18°30'N
18°20'N

Diving in the British Virgin Islands

The BVI offers an incredibly diverse selection of diving environments, which in turn attract an astounding mix of marine life. There are dive sites throughout the territory, with the largest concentration of these around the protected islands and cays south of Tortola. You'll find many healthy underwater gardens abundant in hard and soft corals. Other sites feature beautiful geological formations, including caverns, overhangs, arches and tunnels. The BVI's location along historic trading routes means that divers can explore shipwreck sites both old and new. There are underwater deserts, as well as seafloor meadows of turtle grass. Protected mangroves foster juveniles, while open-water sites host large passing pelagics.

Tropical fish abound on most reefs, making the area a macrophotographer's utopia. Of the larger animals, many rays are often seen—mantas make occasional surprise appearances. Dolphins are common. Divers sometimes encounter sharks, though the population is not large. In recent years, some lucky divers have spotted whale sharks, but this is a rare treat. Between February and April you will very likely hear—and may see—humpback whales, which come to the BVI to breed.

Logistically, diving in the BVI is generally a stress-free affair. Local operators emphasize service and safety, while managing to keep things simple. You'll usually dive with a guide from a large, comfortable vessel. It is also possible to rent a boat and gear to head out on your own. Since the territory's dive industry depends heavily on discerning U.S. divers, all equipment is maintained to U.S. standards, and all instructors belong to one or more of the internationally recognized diving associations, usually PADI, NAUI, SSI or BSAC. Operators belong to the BVI Dive Operators Association, which self-imposes regulations to maintain standards. As at any responsible dive destination, all operators will ask for a valid C-card from a recognized agency.

One convenient option is rendezvous diving, a service developed here in the mid-1980s to cater to the yachting diver. This means that in addition to boarding the dive boat from the dock, you can also be picked up from your anchored yacht. This flexible approach to picking up guests has turned rendezvous diving into a local industry standard.

The BVI offers very few shore dives, mainly because of the lack of good roads leading to the water's edge and the general availability of boats. With few exceptions, all sites are moored, meaning there is almost no drift diving. Sites tend to be relatively shallow—virtually all stay above 90ft (27m). Most sites lie less than 30 minutes from dive operator bases, though extra time may be spent getting everything organized and picking up rendezvous divers from their vessels. A few sites are more re-mote—these excursions may be treated as full-day outings and may include a rest stop on a pristine beach.

At most sites, moderate sea conditions prevail. A handful of sites are exposed to easterly breezes and may roll a little. Though visibility varies from day to day, it is usually between 70 and 100ft (21 and 31m). On good days at some sites, vis-ibility can reach as high as 150ft (46m), but a plankton bloom can drop visibility to 40ft (12m) or less.

At times, extremely good visibility is accompanied by strong currents. These are often surface currents that subside as you go deeper, but you may sometimes encounter se-rious currents at exposed sites. Your dive guide will determine if conditions are safe enough to dive. Drift diving is done occa-sionally (though rarely) in the BVI. If diving inde-pendently (*always* with a buddy), take caution not to drift far from the site and never fight the power of a strong current. It is best to abort your dive early if you discover that the conditions are too extreme.

Soper's Hole is a good dive base on Tortola's West End.

Certification

All BVI dive operators offer complete training programs, from introductory classes through divemaster certification courses. Some operators have more staff than oth-ers and therefore can be more flexible in supplying this training on demand.

While it is possible to get certified here, the BVI is not an especially popular spot to learn how to dive—the majority of visiting divers arrive already certified and require no additional training. Some divers do their classroom work at home and complete their Open Water checkout dives in the BVI. Refresher courses are available for certified divers who haven't been under in a while.

Another option is to take an introductory course (sometimes called a Resort Course or a Discover Scuba Course), which introduces a novice to the wonders of diving within a few hours. This is not a certification program—it allows a non-diver to experience scuba under the close supervision of an instructor. It is best to arrange for classes or checkout dives ahead of time. All major dive associations are represented here, and many instructors are certified by multiple agencies.

Snorkeling

Excellent snorkeling spots are found throughout the BVI. Many of the islands offer good snorkeling from shore. Take sensible precautions and do not snorkel off beaches where surf is present—you won't see much, and you could get caught in strong currents.

Snorkeling around the larger islands is good, with little or no runoff to bring down visibility, but the best snorkel spots are around the outer islands. You can join a daysail or go along with a dive boat. Guides on board will help you make the best of your experience. If you prefer to head out on your own, you can charter a boat for the day or afternoon. (See Listings for more information on chartering a boat.)

Live-Aboards

Live-aboards can be a comfortable and efficient alternative to land-based diving in the BVI. Your vessel is your hotel, restaurant, dive boat and entertainment center for the duration of your trip. The live-aboard option is best for divers who

Top 10 BVI Snorkel Spots

Following are 10 of the BVI's best snorkeling sites, listed in alphabetical order:

The Baths: Virgin Gorda's world-class destination offers gin-clear water, large boulders, small caverns, plenty of marine life and the most beautiful natural pool of water in the territory.

Brewers Bay: Just offshore from one of Tortola's most popular beaches, this easily accessible reef site features a menagerie of fish and bountiful coral life.

The Caves: Three large caves on Norman Island feature shallow waters and many small fish, which in turn attract larger predators.

Cistern Point: You'll see multicolored fish all along Cooper Island's beach and rocky, coral-covered point.

Dry Rocks East: Cooper Island's top shallow dive and snorkel site offers lots of fish activity and, at times, challenging conditions.

Eustatia Sound: Virgin Gorda's shallow northern sound is home to scuttled 18th-century cannons, a pristine reef and hunting eagle rays.

The Indians: This group of pinnacles north of Norman Island is a popular fish-watching spot.

Jellyfish Lagoon: Surrounded by mangroves, Tortola's Prospect Reef is home to hundreds of upsidedown jellyfish and other marine creatures.

Loblolly Bay: Snorkeling is just one of the many natural charms of Anegada's north side, which boasts 24 miles (39km) of pristine beaches.

RMS *Rhone* – Stern: Although most of the famed shipwreck is in deep water, the stern section is shallow—the bronze propeller, rudder, drive shaft and aft mast are visible from the surface.

would like to maximize their dive time and who wish to explore dive sites that are otherwise difficult or impossible to access, such as Horseshoe Reef near Anegada. There are currently several live-aboard dive vessels in the BVI. See the Listings section for details.

Dive Site Icons

The symbols at the beginning of each dive site description provide a quick summary of some of the following characteristics present at each site:

 Good snorkeling or free-diving site.

 Remains or partial remains of a wreck can be seen at this site.

 Sheer wall or drop-off.

 Deep dive. Features of this dive occur in water deeper than 90ft (27m).

 Strong currents may be encountered at this site.

 Strong surge (the horizontal movement of water caused by waves) may be encountered at this site.

 Drift dive. Because of strong currents and/or difficulty in anchoring, a drift dive is recommended at this site.

 Beach/shore dive. This site can be accessed from shore.

 Poor visibility. The site often has visibility of less than 40ft (12m).

 Caves are a prominent feature of this site. Only experienced cave divers should explore inner cave areas.

 Marine preserve. Special regulations apply in this area.

Pisces Rating System for Dives & Divers

The dive sites in this book are rated according to the following diver skill-level rating system. These are not absolute ratings but apply to divers at a particular time, diving at a particular place. For instance, someone unfamiliar with prevailing conditions might be considered a novice diver at one dive area, but an intermediate diver at another, more familiar location.

Novice: A novice diver should be accompanied by an instructor, divemaster or advanced diver on all dives. A novice diver generally fits the following profile:
◆ basic scuba certification from an internationally recognized certifying agency
◆ dives infrequently (less than one trip a year)
◆ logged fewer than 25 total dives
◆ little or no experience diving in similar waters and conditions
◆ dives no deeper than 60ft (18m)

Intermediate: An intermediate diver generally fits the following profile:
◆ may have participated in some form of continuing diver education
◆ logged between 25 and 100 dives
◆ dives no deeper than 130ft (40m)
◆ has been diving in similar waters and conditions within the last six months

Advanced: An advanced diver generally fits the following profile:
◆ advanced certification
◆ has been diving for more than two years and logged over 100 dives
◆ has been diving in similar waters and conditions within the last six months

Regardless of your skill level, you should be in good physical condition and know your limitations. If you are uncertain of your own level of expertise for a particular site, ask the advice of a local dive instructor. He or she is best qualified to assess your abilities based on the site's prevailing dive conditions. Ultimately, however, you must decide if you are capable of making a particular dive, a decision that should take into account your level of training, recent experience and physical condition, as well as the conditions at the site. Remember that conditions can change at any time, even during a dive.

Northwest Dive Sites

Dive sites in the northwest—around the islands of Tortola, Jost Van Dyke and adjacent cays—tend to be isolated and exposed. It is this exposure and relative distance from populated areas that make diving in this area attractive to those looking for a bit of a challenge. The northwest is a good departure from the more commonly dived sites to the south. Many of the sites in this area are diveable only during the calmer summer months, when wind and northern swells die down.

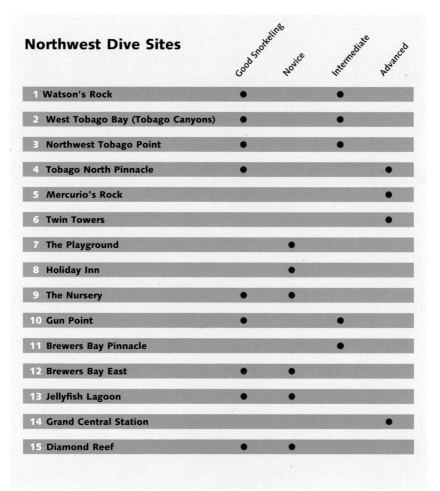

Northwest Dive Sites	Good Snorkeling	Novice	Intermediate	Advanced
1 Watson's Rock	●		●	
2 West Tobago Bay (Tobago Canyons)	●		●	
3 Northwest Tobago Point	●		●	
4 Tobago North Pinnacle	●			●
5 Mercurio's Rock				●
6 Twin Towers				●
7 The Playground		●		
8 Holiday Inn		●		
9 The Nursery	●	●		
10 Gun Point	●		●	
11 Brewers Bay Pinnacle			●	
12 Brewers Bay East	●	●		
13 Jellyfish Lagoon	●	●		
14 Grand Central Station				●
15 Diamond Reef	●	●		

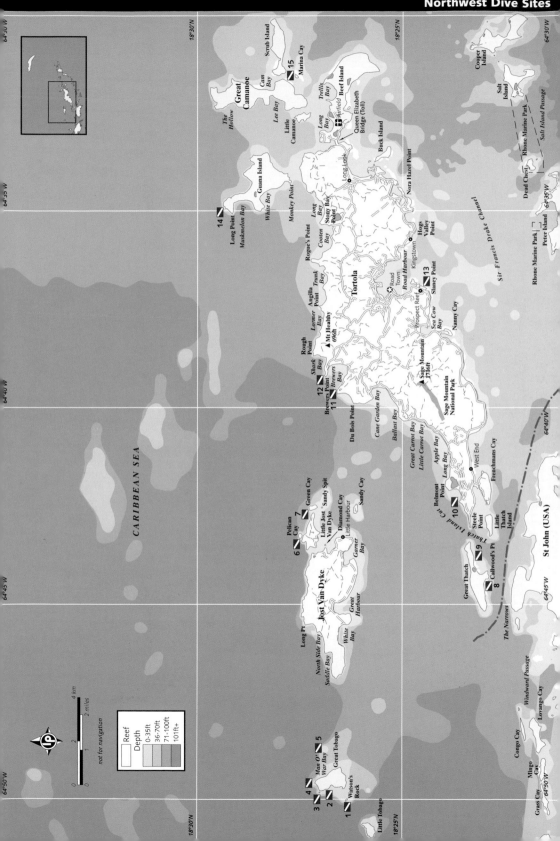

Tobago Cays

The westernmost islands in the BVI, Great Tobago, Little Tobago and tiny Watson's Rock are deserted spots offering no real beach access to the land explorer. These are exposed to north swells, but their western lee sides offer protection from the easterly winds and relatively calm seas for anchoring. This is some of the most isolated diving in the BVI, and few operators travel to these sites regularly, making them attractive to those looking for new places to explore. Conditions in this area can change quickly—if you venture out on your own, be sure to take necessary precautions, including carrying a working VHF radio.

1 Watson's Rock

From the surface, Watson's Rock appears smaller than it really is. Like an iceberg, only the tip—which rises about 90ft above the surface—is visible. The rest of the rock's massive body lies below the surface. The safest places around the rock to dive are the northwest and southwest sides.

On the northwest side, a few offshore pinnacles lie close to the main rock. A highlight of this dive is a large encrusted archway that starts in about 15ft and rises close to the surface. The southwest side features several enormous boulders leading to a large intact field of sea fans

Location: Southwest of Great Tobago

Depth Range: 10-55ft (3-17m)

Access: Boat

Expertise Rating: Intermediate

and gorgonians. Deep sandy canyons separate each boulder from its neighbor.

Arguably, there are more pillar-coral colonies at this site than at any other site in the BVI. All are large and healthy,

Watson's Rock is part of the Tobago Cays, one of the least dived areas of the territory.

Have Calves, Will Travel

Each year, between January and mid-March, humpback whales migrate through BVI waters. Abundant food draws these endangered whales to the North Atlantic in the summertime, while the warmer Caribbean waters lure them south to breed in the winter. The humpback's gestation period is a full year—the female mates one winter and returns to give birth and mate again the following winter. The humpback's cues to move along come from currents, water temperature, length of day, angle of the sun and underwater topography across thousands of miles.

At 45 to 50ft (14 to 15m) long and weighing 35 to 40 U.S. tons (32 to 36 metric tons), adult humpbacks are rather visible visitors. Boaters often spot the whales spouting, "spyhopping" (popping their heads up for a look around), slapping the water with their pectoral fins and flukes, or even breaching—throwing their massive bodies belly up completely out of the water, then crashing headfirst back into the depths. Watch for the Atlantic species' distinctive all-white pectoral fins. Before making deep dives, the whales roll forward, bringing their tails vertically clear of the water.

Divers are often serenaded by this singing whale, whose world-famous vocalizations echo for miles through the water column in songs lasting from 5 to 20 minutes or more. But don't expect close encounters. Nursing humpbacks are naturally wary of human contact, and most commercial operators in the BVI respect an unwritten code of privacy, keeping a good distance from the whales.

with plenty of gobies to take up cleaning-station duties. Lots of blue chromis—both adults and juveniles—live within the pillars. Stay alert for passing schools of fish, which zoom in and out of view. Schools of juvenile Atlantic spadefish pass swiftly by as hundreds of friendly brown chromis fill the water column.

If you dive here during the winter (February to April), you'll likely hear humpback whale songs quite clearly. They are much more easily heard at these offshore sites than at sites in the southern areas. It is often possible to catch sight of a whale breaching or slapping its tail between surface intervals.

2 West Tobago Bay (Tobago Canyons)

This is another little-dived site on Great Tobago's west side. The terrain here drops quickly to a coral-filled bottom at 90ft and below. Look for coral heads with many sea rods and plenty of large sponges. Small blue sponges keep company with large barrel sponges. An array of marine tenants—including crab, shrimp and tiny blennies—occupy the available spaces inside and outside these delicate formations.

Though there are not as many boulders on the west side as there are to the

Location: West of Great Tobago

Depth Range: 15-90ft (4.6-27m)

Access: Boat

Expertise Rating: Intermediate

northwest, the number of fish remains high. You'll see triggerfish, big schools of blue runners and many large barracuda, which hover in the midwater awaiting their prey. The grouper population, though shy, is prolific compared to other sites in the territory.

During a dive here, Sue Thompson, one of the islands' most respected dive guides and instructors, saw the largest nurse shark she had ever seen. She measured the sleeping beast at around 15ft. Though nurse sharks are common throughout the Virgin Islands, specimens that large are rare.

As at all the sites around the Tobago Cays, keep an eye out for poor weather, currents and swells. A sudden rain squall can arrive quickly at any time of year. These weather fronts are preceded by lots of wind. They usually pass quickly and leave only a little rain and a cool breeze behind. If you're diving independently, be sure to always leave someone onboard when you go under. This is no place to be marooned.

3　Northwest Tobago Point

At this site, truck-sized boulders lead to a rubble field at about 90ft. Many undercuts and small caves lead to a sandy bottom. The principal reef lies in shallow water—about 30 to 40ft—but drops away quickly as you head out to sea.

Northwest Tobago Point is one of the BVI's deepest dives. To make the most

Location: Northwest of Great Tobago

Depth Range: 20-90ft (6-27m)

Access: Boat

Expertise Rating: Intermediate

Blue chromis find protection from the area's currents among towering pillar corals.

of your bottom time, try to stay shallow. If you do venture into deeper waters, be sure to return to the area around the rock before surfacing so you don't get caught in the near-surface currents, which could whisk you out to the open seas.

Begin your dive in the deeper section. At about 80ft you'll encounter a healthy soft-coral forest made up of wire corals, bushy black corals and other soft coral trees common only on the BVI's deeper reefs. As you work your way up to the shallows, you'll pass pillar corals and some large elkhorn corals. Sponges of all types, including barrel and tube sponges, dot the entire landscape.

During your dive, be sure to keep an eye on the open sea for pelagic life. Observant divers have spotted eagle rays, mantas and sharks passing by. If silversides are in full force, tuna and tarpon may arrive to feed.

Staghorn corals are common in shallow waters throughout the territory.

4 Tobago North Pinnacle

Just off the north peninsula of Tobago, there is a small pinnacle that rises from about 80ft to about 8ft from the surface. A channel separates the pinnacle from the island itself.

There are many fish species found here, including sunshinefish, a type of chromis. During its juvenile stage, the upper half of the sunshinefish's body is an iridescent yellow. Adults, in contrast, have an olive-brown coloration. During

Location: North of Great Tobago

Depth Range: 8-80ft (2.4-24m)

Access: Boat

Expertise Rating: Advanced

summer, clouds of silversides dot this coastline, attracting ever-hungry tarpon.

5 Mercurio's Rock

Even in the best of conditions, Mercurio's Rock is difficult to find. This submerged mount lies in the middle of nowhere and has no mooring, so unless you know the area, you'll have to go with a knowledgeable guide. Because of its remote offshore location, Mercurio's Rock is considered an advanced site and will appeal to adventurous, skilled divers.

Location: .6 mile (1km) east of Tobago

Depth Range: 6-60ft (1.8-18m)

Access: Boat

Expertise Rating: Advanced

Underwater, the three peaks forming the mass of the seamount come to within 15ft of the surface. The seamount is covered at all levels with corals and soft sponges. Permanent residents include lobsters, and in the evenings you'll see sleeping turtles. The site features plenty of rocky crevices and overhangs, but a main highlight is a 100ft long tunnel large enough to allow a diver to swim through. Inside, schools of glassy sweepers and other fish abound.

The site offers a wealth of marine life, from schooling pelagics to the occasional encounter with a large beast. A few years ago, while on the surface after a dive, I had an intimate encounter with a 200lb loggerhead turtle. Confusing me for a mate, the turtle offered me an unexpected rear embrace—poor vision, but good taste I'd like to think!

Though most operators don't come here on a regular basis, if you have the proper experience you should try to entice your operator to break the routine by bringing you here. With a little persuasion, even the most jaded divemaster can enjoy this wonderful site.

Loggerhead turtles mate at the water's surface—the female will later head ashore to lay her eggs.

Jost Van Dyke

West of Tortola, Jost Van Dyke is a well-known sailor's hangout. The island has some of the most beautiful beaches in the territory. The small, quaint restaurants and bars that dot the few bays have given the island an international reputation as a barefoot party place. The atmosphere here is ultra-casual, offering the sounds and smells of the old-time Caribbean. Jost doesn't have any dive operators—these sites are accessed from Tortola's west end.

Jost's many large and small bays offer protection from wind and weather, allowing silversides to congregate in large masses. Look for black shapes that look like oil slicks contrasting with a bay's clear bottom. Also look for bird activity—this is a telltale sign of the fish that lie below.

The area around Jost Van Dyke is dotted with small islands and cays—Green Cay, Sandy Cay, Sandy Spit and Little Jost Van Dyke. These make great daytrip destinations and offer excellent snorkeling and shallow-water diving.

Tiny Sandy Spit provides all the idyllic elements of a secluded desert-island paradise.

6 Twin Towers

Not far north of Little Jost Van Dyke is Pelican Cay; west of this small cay lies the Twin Towers dive site. Twin Towers is named for two impressive monoliths that rise up from about 90ft, separated by a rubble bottom.

Location: North of Little Jost Van Dyke

Depth Range: 40-90ft (12-27m)

Access: Boat

Expertise Rating: Advanced

The abundance of marine life around the towers varies between seasons. In summer, when the waters are calmer, you'll see huge groups of silversides and tarpon. In winter the surface tends to be turbulent, with the north swells in full force, so there are fewer large congregations of fish. Divers report sightings of an individual jewfish at this site. Jewfish—a large type of grouper that can reach as much as 8ft long—are considered rare in BVI waters after years of overfishing devastated their population. Mantas are also occasionally seen in the area.

Twin Towers lies exposed to open ocean, making it an advanced site. Facing north is an advantage if you are looking for the larger pelagics. The bottom is quite deep, so check it out at the beginning of your dive, but be sure to follow your dive plan. Spend the greater part of your time in the shallower area. Here you'll find sea fans, creolefish, yellowtail snappers and many wrasse species. Look for the occasional tuna passing by in the open water.

Nurse sharks (shown here with an attached remora) tend to be most active at night.

7 | The Playground

On the north side of Green Cay, The Playground is a surprisingly rewarding dive for such an easy site. The main attraction here is a large boulder field just north of the mooring in about 30ft. The boulders are covered in marine growth and attract an abundance of marine life, which finds refuge between the rocks.

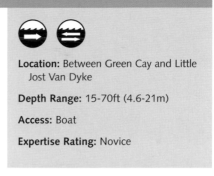

Location: Between Green Cay and Little Jost Van Dyke

Depth Range: 15-70ft (4.6-21m)

Access: Boat

Expertise Rating: Novice

You'll find many gobies here. Look for the elusive green-banded goby—it has a distinctive red stripe running along its snout and vertical light-green stripes along its green body. It lives in shallow water, resting under small rocks, sea urchins and sponges. Other gobies found here include the colon goby—distinguished by a pair of spots on the base of its dorsal fin—and the bridled goby.

As long as there is no north swell, The Playground is an easy, calm dive.

When the surf breaks in the shallows, it looks like gathering storm clouds momentarily blocking the sunlight. Tarpon hunting near the surface take advantage of the camouflage provided by the confusion of water and air.

Nearby, just south of Green Cay, the small island of **Sandy Spit** is as idyllic as islands get. Though it is not part of the dive site, it makes a perfect snorkeling stop for divers in the area.

A brittle star embraces the sponge it calls home.

Great Thatch Island

Great Thatch and its smaller neighbor Little Thatch are just a mile or so west of Tortola's west end. Great Thatch is barren but has a wonderful natural bay for day anchoring and a handful of novice dive sites. Little Thatch has been tastefully developed into a small upscale resort.

8 | Holiday Inn

Holiday Inn is on the south side of Great Thatch Island. Although the site is exposed to the wind and currents of the Sir Francis Drake Channel, it's considered a novice site in part because it is protected from the northern swells.

The dive is centered around a semi-vertical drop that leads out in the direction of the channel. The bottom is dotted with pockets of hard coral and scattered soft corals. Schools of fish congregate in different areas—look for grunts, highhats, spotted drums, parrotfish and many other reef dwellers.

Location: South of Great Thatch Island

Depth Range: 40-60ft (12-18m)

Access: Boat

Expertise Rating: Novice

Because the site is an exposed shallow reef, visibility is relatively low, about 40 to 50ft. The tradeoff is that there are a lot of fish, with many different species found in this one easy-to-dive area. Divers looking for macrophotographic opportunities in particular will not be disappointed.

Because overfishing has depleted their numbers, extra-large schools of grunts are an unusual treat.

9 | The Nursery

Location: Great Thatch Bay

Depth Range: 15-45ft (4.6-14m)

Access: Boat

Expertise Rating: Novice

The Nursery is considered a novice site because it is shallow and relatively easy going. Access is easy, surface conditions are very calm and the site is protected from most weather. As at most shallow BVI reefs, visibility can sometimes drop but tends to clear up quickly. A multitude of medium-sized coral heads are surrounded by sandy patches, which lead to larger patches in the deeper areas. A typical array of soft and hard corals is found throughout the site.

At night, the relatively barren landscape transforms into a garden as coral polyps come out to feed in the gentle current. Your dive light will attract myriad creatures, so be prepared. Night dives here bring you face-to-face with squid, octopus, lobsters, crab and shrimp.

As the site name implies, you can find just about every juvenile species of fish in the book. You also have the added benefit of being in shallow water, so you can spend plenty of time searching around for the little guys. Expect to find many species of blenny, wrasse, snapper, grunt and goby, as well as other members of the tropical reef community, from flashy juveniles to hungry adults.

Although this is a novice site, experienced divers can still enjoy it. Photographers in particular should not miss this great opportunity to shoot so many species in their different stages of development, all in one shallow site. The Nursery is a macrophotographer's oasis.

The site can also be enjoyed by snorkelers, who can enjoy the shallower sections close to shore. Always try to stay alert for the possibile arrival of eagle rays and other midwater creatures that may approach as you drift silently on the surface.

The juvenile spotted drum (top) does not gain its spots until maturity (bottom).

Tortola

There is limited diving off Tortola itself, though the few regularly visited sites in the north and an unusual lagoon on the south coast are worth a visit.

Tortola is the main hub of the BVI, and the majority of all sailing charter companies and support services are based here. The island's dive operators are spread out along the south coast. Tortola's north coast is an emerging dive area, which has only recently become popular with dive operators based out of the west end. In search of new dive sites closer to the west end's main commercial area of Soper's Hole, divemasters have discovered many good sites accessible only by boat. There are many more to be found—every peninsula and exposed rock on the north side is a potential first-class dive site.

With sites around Brewers Bay, Tortola's north shore is one of the BVI's emerging dive areas.

10 Gun Point

Gun Point is one of the best snorkeling sites on Tortola's remote north coast. The site's bottom is punctuated with scattered boulders surrounded by beautiful soft corals, including sea fans and sea whips. Near shore, the depth ranges from 10 to 25ft. Rocks, cracks on the seabed and ledges lead to the point on Smuggler's Cove. As you snorkel the

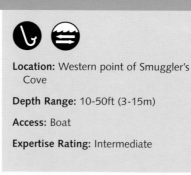

Location: Western point of Smuggler's Cove

Depth Range: 10-50ft (3-15m)

Access: Boat

Expertise Rating: Intermediate

shallows, you'll be accompanied by swarms of fish, including silver porgies, highhats and spotted drums, as well as lobsters. Also expect to see overwhelmingly large schools of silversides, which are chased up and down this coast by the ubiquitous tarpon.

Farther out, there is a drop that begins at about 40ft. During a recent survey, more than 93 species of fish and invertebrates were counted in waters below 40ft. You are likely to find nurse sharks sleeping under ledges. Look for tiny tuna, which sometimes come close to shore in small schools, occasionally followed by a larger predator. Keep an eye on the blue water for the occasional hawksbill turtle.

Predatory jacks come to the area to feast on massive schools of silversides.

11 Brewers Bay Pinnacle

Because this site is completely exposed, it is generally a summer-only dive site, unless you happen upon a winter day with no northern swells. The mooring is found just outside of one of Tortola's most beautiful natural bay beaches, which hosts the island's only campground. As you approach the bay from the winding hillside, you can clearly see the tip of Brewers Point. The rough on-land terrain is a direct reflection of what lies underwater.

The underwater pinnacles just off Brewers Point lie in 70 to 80ft, with the

Location: West side of Brewers Bay

Depth Range: 20-80ft (6-24m)

Access: Boat

Expertise Rating: Intermediate

top coming to within 20ft of the surface. Visibility here can be poor by Caribbean standards, averaging about 60ft. You'll want to avoid this dive in rainy weather, as the site is near a large river basin that flows only during the wet season. If there's a lot of constant rain—quite unusual here—runoff spills into the bay and may affect visibility.

As at many sites on Tortola's northwest side, silversides and tarpon often dominate the scene during the summer months, while sightings of mantas and other pelagics are possible year-round.

This is also shark territory, so keep an eye out for the stealthy creatures. Reef, lemon and bull sharks frequent Tortola's north side, particularly east of Brewers Bay, an area that includes the aptly named Shark Bay.

12 Brewers Bay East

On the eastern peninsula of Brewers Bay lies a dive site that resembles a deeper version of the better-known Baths dive and snorkel spot on Virgin Gorda. Here, large boulders are scattered all over the bottom, creating a field of swim-throughs. There is also an inshore reef you can explore, but the dive's best areas lie between and around these large boulders, where fish find refuge.

Look along the sandy bottom for the elusive and extremely beautiful flying gurnard. Growing to no more than 18 inches long, this unusual fish is impressive to watch. It has huge fanlike pectoral fins, which it uses to glide just above the sand. Like a rancher on a horse, the gurnard rounds up small fish until it manages to contain one within its wings

Location: Eastern tip of Brewers Bay

Depth Range: 10-70ft (3-21m)

Access: Boat

Expertise Rating: Novice

and devour it whole. The iridescent blue lines and dots on the gurnard's wings are difficult to see unless the fish is fully lit. When its pectoral fins are folded in, the fish perches up and seems to walk on its ventral fins.

Another rarity that thrives here is the hard-to-find longlure frogfish. The frogfish sits motionless, camouflaging itself among soft sponges and rubble. This clever fish waits patiently, using a false lure to attract prey to its large mouth. Frogfish vary in color from pink to yellow or orange and range in size from 3 to 8 inches.

When silversides are present, stay above 15ft to watch the action. You'll find that the site transforms into a potpourri of marine life, with tarpon, jacks, Bermuda chub and

If disturbed, the gurnard will spread its wings and "fly" away.

anchovies, as well as pelicans and boobies, intermingling in a dance of shapes and light. The outcome of their encounter is predetermined—a few silversides will survive to carry on the species, while the majority will become a feast for the larger members of the food chain.

13 | Jellyfish Lagoon

This small lagoon on the outskirts of Road Town is not an official dive site. Accessed from shore only, the site lies literally 10ft from Drake's Highway, a two-lane road that stretches along Tortola's south coast.

Location: South shore of Tortola

Depth Range: Surface-6ft (1.8m)

Access: Shore

Expertise Rating: Novice

The shallow lagoon is like a living laboratory and is a great spot for divers who take interest in the biological and ecological sides of diving. Jellyfish Lagoon is a favorite spot for macrophotographers, who snap shots of the hundreds of upsidedown jellyfish that congregate in the shadow of a small mangrove island. The jellyfish lie motionless on the bottom with their arms reaching up toward the surface. The rays of sunlight streaming through accelerate the growth of zooxanthellae, a single-celled algae that lives on the jellyfish's tissue in a symbiotic relationship.

The water temperature of the lagoon is usually a few degrees warmer than the surrounding ocean. The lagoon is shallow, so most visitors will only want to snorkel. If you're visiting as a serious photographer, diving gear will allow you a bit more flexibility. In either case, you'll want to be careful of the jellyfish's mild sting. If disturbed, the jellyfish will release stinging cells. The sting is not serious, but may be felt on the skin for a few minutes. Use a light protective hood and gloves if possible. Generally, as long as you don't pick up the creature from the bottom, you should be fine. It is also better to stay upcurrent from the jellyfish—that way, if the creature is disturbed, the stinging cells will drift away from you.

On the far site of the lagoon is a small mangrove island. Hundreds of juvenile fish make this shallow root system home before heading out to inhabit the coral reefs of outer islands. Here you can see all the species found in other parts of the BVI, but in miniature.

Many upsidedown jellyfish inhabit this lagoon.

Guana Island

Guana Island is a ritzy private resort island just off the northeastern tip of Tortola. Guests include celebrities and ordinary people with deep pockets. Guana is a beautiful island with wonderful natural features, including many iguanas and a small pond with flamingos. Roaming inland from the beach—which, like all BVI beaches, is public—is prohibited unless you're a guest of the resort.

14 | Grand Central Station

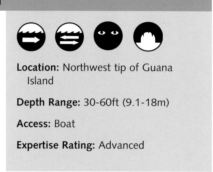

This large cave on the north side of Guana Island has two entrances—a large entrance on one side and a small slit at ground level on the other side. The slit is large enough for a diver with gear to enter. From the inside, both entrances are clearly visible. You will see a large X on the north side wall above the water's surface, marking the smaller entrance.

Location: Northwest tip of Guana Island

Depth Range: 30-60ft (9.1-18m)

Access: Boat

Expertise Rating: Advanced

Inside, the cave rapidly expands to a vaulted ceiling similar to that of the famed New York City train station. Inside, you'll swim in about 40ft. Overhead, you'll see a 3ft high air pocket, formed over time from the air released by divers. Definitely do not breathe the stale air—if you stick your head up into the air pocket, be sure to keep your regulator in.

Cave inhabitants include lobsters, crab, shrimp and other creatures of the dark. Outside the larger entrance you'll find large boulders and corals that form the north shore of Guana Island. In this area, silversides and tarpon dominate the scene. Look out into the open water to glimpse an Atlantic manta ray or two.

Diving here should only be attempted in the best of conditions. Wind, surge and northern swells are always a problem, anchoring is treacherous and visibility can be low. Despite the difficulties, Grand Central Station remains a wonderful and unusual place to explore.

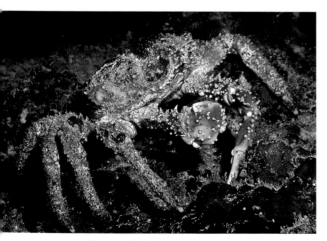

Channel-clinging crabs forage mainly at night.

Great Camanoe Island

Great Camanoe is another private island boasting some of the BVI's most exclusive residences. It is accessible by boat only—the island's version of a parking lot is a small boat marina where residents pull up to offload their guests and supplies.

To the southeast, Marina Cay is home to a small restaurant and bar operated by the folks from Pusser's, Tortola's legendary watering hole. Marina Cay has a long romantic history—stories of love and survival were made into the 1958 Sidney Poitier film *Virgin Island* and Robb White's island memoir *Two on the Isle*.

There is excellent snorkeling in the shallow waters just off Marina Cay's beach. Eagle rays come in to feed here, and many small juvenile fish take refuge in the less-than-6ft waters. Dive BVI runs an air-filling station on Marina Cay.

15 | Diamond Reef

Diamond Reef lies between Great Camanoe Island and its neighbor, Marina Cay. Because the reef dips quickly, following the natural contours of the land, this is a great place for new divers to get acquainted with the area. Underwater, the coral dips gently to a sandy bottom at 60ft. The site is home to a good population of fish, as well as a garden eel colony.

Location: Southeast of Great Camanoe

Depth Range: 20-60ft (6-18m)

Access: Boat

Expertise Rating: Novice

A gentle current often flows from south to north, allowing for a drift dive. It's not a serious current, but it's enough to carry you along slowly in one direction. When you surface, you should be parallel to shore, just north of where you started.

Visibility can be low by BVI standards but remains well within enjoyment level. Waters here are usually calm. The site is easily accessed by dinghy from the popular anchorage at Marina Cay, a few hundred yards east.

The sharknosed goby is one of several cleaning species in the BVI.

Southwest Dive Sites

The southwest is one of the most dived areas in the BVI—and with good reason. There are many fabulous sites here within a relatively small area. The area's one filling station is based on Peter Island. Otherwise, you must bring all air out with you. Most of the dive operators that come here are based out of Road Town or Nanny Cay (off Tortola's south coast). The area is dotted with picturesque islands and cays. Dives sites are varied and include reef, wreck and open-water sites.

Southwest Dive Sites

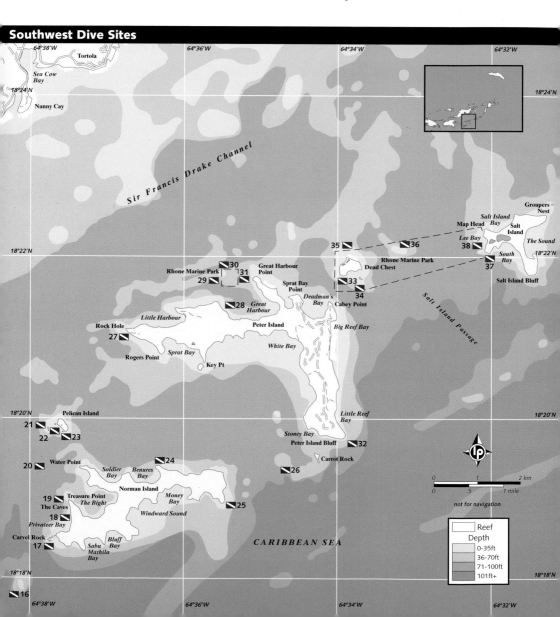

Southwest Dive Sites

	Good Snorkeling	Novice	Intermediate	Advanced
16 Santa Monica Rock				●
17 Angel Reef	●		●	
18 Sandy Ledges	●	●		
19 The Caves	●	●		
20 Ring Dove Rock		●	●	
21 The Indians	●	●		
22 Pelican Reef		●		
23 Rainbow Canyon		●		
24 Spyglass Wall	●	●		
25 Brown Pants			●	
26 Carrot Shoals			●	
27 Black Forest	●		●	
28 Randy's Reef	●	●		
29 *Rhone*'s Anchor			●	
30 Truck Reef			●	
31 *Fearless & Willy T*			●	
32 Shark Point			●	
33 Dead Chest West		●		
34 Painted Walls	●	●		
35 Coral Gardens	●	●		
36 Blonde Rock			●	
37 *Rhone* Reef			●	
38 RMS *Rhone*	●	●	●	

Norman Island

This uninhabited cactus-covered island is home to many peaceful, secluded anchorages. Norman Island has more than its share of pirate lore attached to it. The last major treasure found here was a century ago, but stories of undiscovered pirate booty still make their way into bar conversation. For divers, however, the real treasure is in the quality and variety of the diving around the island.

Among the nondiving attractions of Norman Island is the *Willy T II*, one of the area's most popular anchorages. A Baltic trader permanently moored at The Bight, she is the only floating bar and restaurant in the BVI, and she makes a great place to pull up for a hamburger and a cold drink. The popular watering hole is known for spontaneous parties and the wild and uninhibited behavior of its clientele. The original *Willy T* (also a floating bar and restaurant) suffered irreparable hurricane damage a few years back and was laid to rest in Peter Island's Great Harbour.

Another of the area's attractions is Clive's Bottle Reef, situated right near the *Willy T II*. In 1991, Clive Petrovich—a local yachtsman, dive instructor and biology professor at BVI Community College—created an artificial reef out of more than 3,000 bottles. The goal of this more-or-less scientific experiment was to see how many fish species could be attracted into a barren area if the right lodging existed. The number of juveniles attracted to this secure habitat is enormous—at last count there were 55 species residing at this one site.

Pirate treasure was discovered in these caves.

Artificial Reefs

Although natural reefs thrive throughout the BVI, over the years many artificial reefs have been placed to encourage the establishment of new coral and fish populations. Observing artificial reefs at different stages of development is one of the best ways for divers to understand reef evolution. Artificial reefs can be made of any foreign object that has been submerged: ship or plane wrecks, "junk" like tires or bottles, and concrete blocks. Even broken-up wrecks with their parts scattered about lend themselves well to marine life inhabitation and are generally worth at least a couple of dives.

The abundance of marine life and coral growth on an artificial reef depends on three main factors:

Location: Reefs (both natural and artificial) provide animals with shelter from the current and predators. Artificial reefs placed in open, sandy areas become oases for the surrounding marine life. Hence, this type of reef tends to feature a denser concentration of marine life than an area on an open coral reef, where there are many more places to find shelter. Artificial reefs in current-swept locations often attract species and juveniles that are otherwise rarely seen. Clive's Bottle Reef is an example of an artificial reef that is successful because of its location in an open area.

Material: Steel generally provides an easy surface for coral to grow on. Rubber and aluminum objects, though they may provide excellent shelter, are more difficult for coral to grow on.

Age: Generally, coral takes at least a few years to establish itself. As the coral becomes more profuse, more and more species are gradually attracted. The longer the object has been underwater, the more populated and interesting the artificial reef becomes. A well-situated artificial reef may, over time, become engulfed by a healthy coral population, rendering the original object unrecognizable.

16 Santa Monica Rock

This underwater rock lies in relative isolation almost a mile southwest of Norman Island. Though Santa Monica Rock is visible from the surface, it doesn't reach close enough to the surface to pose a navigational threat.

Underwater, the rock slopes slowly on all sides to a hard rocky bottom. Deep overhangs and other formations offer protection to lobsters, crab and schools of grunts and squirrelfish. Because Santa Monica Rock lies well offshore, it also benefits from the traffic of larger pelagics that cruise the area. Barracuda, bar jacks, blue runners, horse-eye jacks and

Location: .8 mile (1.3km) southwest of Norman Island

Depth Range: 20-70ft (6-21m)

Access: Boat

Expertise Rating: Advanced

Atlantic spadefish are commonly seen, as is the occasional manta or shark.

This site should only be dived in the best of weather and with a dive operator. It is exposed to wind and, on occasion, to unpredictable currents. During the winter, expect to see larger-than-normal swells here. If diving independently, be sure to leave someone aboard your vessel in case a diver drifts away. Also, make sure your mooring line is securely fastened.

A colorful, solitary queen angelfish meets up with a group of grunts.

17 | Angel Reef

With a number of shallow canyons rising to the surface, a coral-and-rock bottom and a seagrass area, this is one of the most prolific and varied sites on Norman. Nudibranchs, blennies, jawfish, soldierfish and an assortment of angelfish are common sights, as are octopuses, southern stingrays, eagle rays and the occasional snake eel. The reef's south side is exposed to open water, luring in the occasional large pelagic for a close encounter. Angel Reef is also a great night

Location: Southwest peninsula of Norman Island

Depth Range: 20-65ft (6-20m)

Access: Boat

Expertise Rating: Intermediate

dive, with squid and sleeping hawksbill turtles found regularly.

The male sailfin blenny unfurls its distinctive fin in a show of territorial behavior or sexual prowess.

Divers commonly spot sailfin blennies in a small sandy patch adjacent to the mooring ball. These fish inhabit holes in rocks. Sailfin blennies are very territorial—if two fish end up as neighbors, each will emerge to display its beautiful sail in a show of sexual prowess, and the pair may get into an outright brawl.

18 Sandy Ledges

This extremely shallow ledge lies about 100ft from Norman Island's west shore. Very shallow and full of the region's most colorful fish species, Sandy Ledges is as close as you get to a tropical fish aquarium in the open ocean. Juveniles and adults mingle under this coral ledge, which works itself back into the bedrock, creating a small cavelike environment. Here small fish find protection from larger predators and seem to thrive.

The ledge is fringed by a sandy bottom, which in deeper water sprouts turtle grass. With three different environments to choose from, you can

Location: Privateer Bay, Norman Island

Depth Range: 5-10ft (1.5-3m)

Access: Boat

Expertise Rating: Novice

expect to see a multitude of species, including some rarer creatures. Look for the goldenhind (a coney in its least common golden phase), goldspotted snake eels and spotted drums (in all stages of development), just to mention a few.

For the underwater photographer, this is a precious site for macro work. It is shallow and calm and has very good visibility, allowing you to work longer and more efficiently in a rich environment. Photographers might want to add a few pounds to their weight belts to stay put on the bottom.

The brilliant goldenhind—a coney in its rare golden phase.

19 The Caves

This busy spot is probably the second-most popular daysail destination in the BVI, after The Baths in Virgin Gorda. It is mainly a snorkeling spot, but divers can enjoy some wonderful times just sitting on the bottom watching out for new species. Three caves penetrate the bedrock of Treasure Point at the waterline. The deepest and most impressive of the trio goes back about 75ft. It was here in 1907 that a Tortola family made the most recent find of the area's great pirate treasures. Though the other two caves are smaller, they offer the same impressive array of marine life.

The water inside the caves is only about 5ft deep, with dry areas above the water level. Bring along a dive light to inspect the crevices along the way. Look for shrimp, tiny lobsters, glassy sweepers and many juvenile fish. You'll usually find silversides in the caves' shallow water. Jacks and other large fish chase the silversides in and out of the caves. The cave areas should be explored by snorkel only.

Look for squid hugging the cave entrances. Along the sponge- and coral-rich vertical wall just outside the cave entrances, you can spend hours tracking

Location: West of Treasure Point, Norman Island

Depth Range: Surface-40ft (12m)

Access: Boat

Expertise Rating: Novice

minuscule creatures such as sea slugs and nudibranchs. These small invertebrates resemble snails without their shells and come in an array of vibrant colors.

For years The Caves has been a popular fish-feeding spot, attracting hundreds of sergeant majors and yellowtail snappers, which congregate for a feast of bread and crackers. They are not shy and may gently nibble your finger. Though the unnatural practice is generally discouraged by both the BVI dive industry and conservationists, fish-feeding at The Caves is unregulated and quite common.

The site is calm and lee of easterly weather conditions. Because it is on the west side of Norman Island, it also experiences some breathtaking sunsets.

A snorkeler makes friends with sergeant majors near the entrance to The Caves.

20 Ring Dove Rock

Halfway between The Indians and The Bight at Norman Island, in the middle of a busy channel, lies this shallow underwater island. Ring Dove Rock is exposed to currents and sailing traffic, so be extra cautious, especially near the surface, where you'll probably spend most of your time.

Here a large oval-shaped rock rises from a sandy bottom to a few feet from the surface. Sharp canyons slice though the rock in various areas. In the deeper areas, large hard corals prevail, while the rock's top and gently sloping sides are covered with sea fans, gorgonians and other soft corals.

The upper crest of the rock bustles with activity, so it's here on the surface

Location: .5 mile (.8km) northwest of Norman Island

Depth Range: 15-70ft (4.6-21m)

Access: Boat

Expertise Rating: Intermediate

that most of the excitement happens. Sergeant majors, jacks and rainbow runners mingle in midcurrent, competing for food. You might be surprised by a school of fish being chased by a hungry barracuda or large jack. Overhangs offer hiding places for lobsters and other shade-loving creatures.

Long and slender, a trumpetfish can hide among gorgonian bushes.

21 The Indians

The Indians is one of the BVI's most popular dive sites. Just off Norman Island, four cone-shaped rocks rise from a depth of 40ft to about 30ft above the surface. Three of the rocks stand together, while the fourth is separated by a narrow channel. The channel is the only way to move between the rocks' east and west sides without circumnavigating the whole conglomerate.

Snorkelers will be happy in the protected pools on the east side of the rocks. Divers start on the rocks' deeper west side, which features a steep rock face. Near the bottom, fish fill the narrow passages, and large sea fans and small corals dot the walls. The maximum depth here is about 50ft. When you cross to the east side of the rocks—whether through the channel or by swimming around—you'll find a completely different dive. The east

Location: West of Pelican Island

Depth Range: Surface-50ft (15m)

Access: Boat

Expertise Rating: Novice

side is much shallower—not more than about 20ft deep.

Look for a small cave full of glassy sweepers to the right of the channel. Farther down the shallow end, you'll find a few large pools. Here, millions of silversides congregate several times a year, usually during the summer and occasionally in the winter. Though you won't usually see tarpon, the site's many jacks manage to keep the schools in check. If you see an abundance of boobies and pelicans on the surface as you approach the site, you'll know that silversides are present. As you continue along the east side, you'll encounter a natural tunnel. About 10ft long, it's large enough to pass through comfortably with your gear. Past the tunnel, the site opens up again, allowing you to continue around the southern tip and back to the west side.

The Indians is considered to be one of the best spots for macro life in the BVI. This is a great place to find and photograph the most minuscule of reef inhabitants, including nudibranchs, blennies and gobies. There are also plenty of shallow corals and abundant tropical fish.

The Indians is an easy dive that attracts experts as well as beginners. The moorings can accommodate at least six vessels, and there is a dinghy area for smaller boats, so the site can sometimes get downright crowded. If you have time on your hands, wait for a group to finish their dive before you enter. Your patience will be rewarded when you have the site to yourself.

The four rocks that make up The Indians dive site attract groups of divers.

22 Pelican Reef

Pelican Reef is just south of Pelican Island, a small island northwest of Norman Island's Water Point. Though you'll find healthy coral formations and plenty of fish life any time of year, a special time to visit is during the annual

Location: South of Pelican Island

Depth Range: 20-45ft (6-14m)

Access: Boat

Expertise Rating: Novice

coral spawning. Each August, seven to 10 days after the full moon, you can watch the corals release their eggs into the current. The eggs are fertilized, settling later on the ocean floor to continue the life cycle of the reef.

The coral spawning event happens throughout the BVI, but Pelican Reef is a particularly good shallow site to watch it unfold. Patience is a virtue when attempting to watch and photograph the actual moment the eggs are released. Luckily, this site lies lee of Pelican Island, so it is protected from the waves and the current.

Bring several tanks for your dive. You can pass the long wait for the spawning—often several hours—by inspecting the healthy coral heads. The spawning usually takes place a few hours after sunset. You'll know when the coral is ready to release the eggs by looking at the polyps—you can actually see the eggs emerging.

Sex & the Coral Reef

While many aspects of coral reproduction remain scientific mysteries, the timing of a coral spawning event is precise. Seven to 10 nights after the first full moon in August, the BVI's reefs explode in an upside-down underwater snowstorm of coral sperm and eggs.

The mass spawning is nature's way of ensuring survival of the species. Depending on the coral species, polyps are either hermaphroditic or produce either eggs or sperm. Upon release, the procreative packets float to the surface, where they separate and mingle. Sometimes the release is slow and steady, other times the surface is thick with slick. The fertilized eggs hatch into larvae, which lead a planktonic existence before settling down on the reef to resume the cycle.

23 Rainbow Canyon

Rainbow Canyon is a favorite with novice divers. It is calm and relatively shallow and has extraordinary coral and marine life. Large coral heads rise from a sandy bottom, and you can also see classic spur-and-groove coral formations with canyons and small overhangs. Spur-and-groove reefs consist of long coral ridges (spurs) separated by valleys

Location: South of Pelican Island

Depth Range: 25-60ft (7.6-18m)

Access: Boat

Expertise Rating: Novice

of sand (grooves). The spurs and grooves usually run in the direction of the prevailing swells.

Expect to find the complete rainbow of colorful fish, including beautiful hamlets in assorted combinations of yellow, blue and purple. Watch for cleaning stations, where small fish dutifully perform the risky task of cleaning the jaws, gills and scales of their much larger clients.

Keep an eye out for scorpionfish camouflaged against the coral. Scorpionfish can be difficult to distinguish from the coral itself—look for the fish's watchful eye. When the scorpionfish is threatened, needles on its dorsal fin are erected and can cause a painful injury if touched or stepped on. Always look closely before you grab a rock, and be careful when walking in shallow waters.

A large colony of garden eels inhabits the sandy field beside the coral heads, in the deeper part of the site. Garden eels live in holes in the sand, usually in large colonies. The eel—which is long and thin, with a coloring of dark-brown to gray—extends out of its burrow to feed on plankton in the current. They are spooked quite easily, retreating into their burrows, so approach slowly and with great patience.

The scorpionfish blends in with surrounding rocks.

24 Spyglass Wall

This is as close to a wall dive as you'll find here in the BVI. Running parallel to Norman Island, a plateau of large coral formations lies in shallow water. A steep drop—from 20 to 60ft—takes you from a coral-rich environment to a deeper, sponge-rich area, before eventually settling to a sandy bottom. You'll see stovepipe sponges, as well as purple, yellow and brown tube sponges. Be sure to look inside the tubes and vases of the sponges for the many creatures that live there. Shrimp and a variety of gobies are common residents, as are bristle stars and yellowline arrow crabs.

Large coral heads and an abundance of tropical fish can be found throughout the site. When schools of silversides are present, expect to see tarpon hunting.

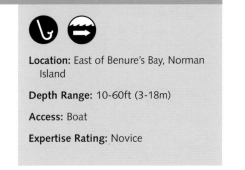

Location: East of Benure's Bay, Norman Island

Depth Range: 10-60ft (3-18m)

Access: Boat

Expertise Rating: Novice

Divers might spot anything from a foot-long mantis shrimp emerging from its burrow to an eagle ray feeding in the shallows. Keep your eyes peeled on the deeper sections for unexpected schools of fish. Since the topography isn't the main draw here, this is a site that can either put you to sleep or provide the dive of your life.

25 Brown Pants

Brown Pants, on Norman's southeastern tip, is a dive that can surprise even the most experienced diver. Open to wind and waves from the east and south, Brown Pants is impossible to attempt in anything but the best of weather. Exposure to the open sea has its rewards—keep your eyes on the open blue water for the occasional manta, shark or other large pelagic. In fact, the site's unusual name most likely came from a diver's unexpected encounter with a very large creature.

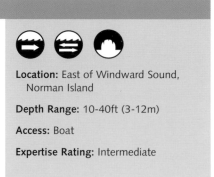

Location: East of Windward Sound, Norman Island

Depth Range: 10-40ft (3-12m)

Access: Boat

Expertise Rating: Intermediate

A cave on the shore side of the mooring ball goes back about 40ft. Shafts of light penetrate into the cave from breaks in the rocky surface. Silversides, glassy sweepers and lobsters abound. Outside of the cave, Brown Pants is best explored close to shore, under the ledges and large rocky formations. Because of its exposure to open seas, corals are not as abundant at this site as at other, more protected sites. The site's few coral patches attract many fish.

Unless conditions are extremely calm, waves break heavily on the surface close to shore. In this tumultuous mix of air, water and marine life, small pockets of juvenile fish congregate to feed on floating food particles. If you are patient, you'll also observe rainbow runners, jacks, mackerel and, from time to time, larger blue-water hunters, which burst through the turbulent water in search of a meal.

Photographers may find both macro and wide-angle opportunities here. Choosing between the two set-ups is sometimes the main challenge—you may wish to bring two cameras down with you.

The cave at this site is accessible only in summer.

Peter Island

Northwest of Norman Island, Peter Island is a private island owned by the U.S. Amway Corporation. It attracts a high-end clientele to its multimillion-dollar resort and marina. The island is dotted with wonderful anchorages and safe harbors. Deadman's Bay, on the island's north side, is one of the most beautiful beaches in the territory. The island's two principal harbors—Great Harbour and Little Harbour—have been used as safe havens for vessels of all sizes for more than 300 years. History has decorated the seafloor with its fair share of large chains and anchors from past eras.

All BVI beaches are public, including those on the otherwise private Peter Island. Visitors can dine at the resort for lunch or dinner and may use the marina facilities. Baskin in the Sun runs a satellite dive operation here with an air-filling station and a nicely appointed dive store and boutique. Randy Keil, the shop's manager and head instructor, is one of the most knowledgeable guides you'll encounter. He's been diving and working in these parts for a long time and knows what he's talking about when it comes to marine life and dive training.

Though Peter Island is private, all BVI beaches—including those at Deadman's Bay—are public.

Blue-Water Diving

Blue-water diving—that is, diving at extremely deep open-water sites—is rising in popularity in the BVI. At blue-water sites, the bottom of the ocean lies far below the sport-diving limit of 130ft (40m). Divers drop to about 40 to 60ft (12 to 18m) and hang on for a drift dive. Since visibility is extraordinary—usually in the 150-to-300ft (45-to-90m) range—the possibility of seeing large pelagics such as marlin, sailfish, large jellyfish and whale sharks is great. Divers in search of tiger sharks descend in cages. Other blue-water attractions include juvenile triggerfish, which congregate just below the surface. From time to time, you'll find sargassum beds—kelp blankets that shelter large numbers of small fish. Encounters with green and leatherback turtles, tuna, mahi-mahi (also known as dorado or dolphinfish) and dolphins are also possible. If underwater photography or video is your thing, the open water is something you should try.

Blue-water diving is new to the BVI, mainly because most visiting divers are relative novices. Ask around at local dive shops to see who is arranging a blue-water excursion. Diving in open water is an unusual approach to the sport and is very different from reef, wall or wreck diving. There is no bottom, as the blue ocean sinks beneath you to unfathomable depths. The boat floats silently above you as you drift slowly along with the current. Blue-water diving is only for the advanced diver and isn't for the faint of heart. In the BVI, most blue-water diving takes place several miles out to sea, south of Peter and Norman Islands. Sea conditions in the summer months are most favorable for this type of diving.

26 | Carrot Shoals

This large underwater rock rises to within 9ft of the surface. It slopes steeply on both sides to a rocky second shelf at about 40ft, before dropping gently to the bottom. As at other exposed sites, Carrot Shoals is prone to high seas and strong currents, which are accentuated by the shoal's long and narrow shape. It should only be dived in favorable conditions.

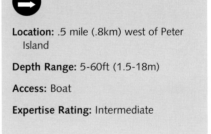

Location: .5 mile (.8km) west of Peter Island

Depth Range: 5-60ft (1.5-18m)

Access: Boat

Expertise Rating: Intermediate

At night, a parrotfish forms its cocoon.

Carrot Shoals is covered in fire coral and other hard corals. A multitude of plankton-eating fish—including the ever-present sergeant majors and jacks—swarm near the surface. As at other offshore sites, pelagic fish come in to feed on a regular basis. Overhangs, undercuts and small caves at the skirt of the rock protect schooling grunts and other fish, as well as eels, turtles, lobsters and other reef inhabitants.

This site deserves more than one dive—preferably at different times of the day—to appreciate the complexity of its changing mini-ecosystem. Like most living communities, a dive site has different periods of activity throughout the day. At Carrot Shoals, late after-noon just before sunset is a favorite time. Though visibility tends to drop slightly, plankton is more abundant, attracting large numbers of plankton-eaters like sergeant majors. These, in turn, attract hunters like barracuda, permit and Afri-can pompano.

27 Black Forest

Black Forest lies just south of Peter Island's pointed west end, where it is protected from most weather. The dive begins under the mooring ball in rela-tively shallow waters where tropical fish and corals abound. Just a few feet out to sea from the mooring, a relatively steep slope brings you to a sandy bot-tom at about 75ft.

Location: Southwest of Peter Island

Depth Range: 15-65ft (4.6-20m)

Access: Boat

Expertise Rating: Intermediate

A forest of large black-coral trees populates the entire slope, earning the site its name. The site is also home to sea fans and a healthy variety of corals. Pockets of fish life—including schools of Caesar, French and bluestriped grunts—hide beneath coral heads, while trumpetfish lie ver-tically among the gorgonians. Look for large groups of hound-fish (a type of needlefish) swimming just below the surface.

At the base of the sloping wall lies a sandy desert. It is empty except for a large colony of gar-den eels that blankets the area. Garden eels are easily spooked and will retreat quickly into their burrows—if you are pa-tient and move slowly, you might be able to get up close. Eagle rays and, more commonly, southern stingrays are also seen in this area.

A large sea fan decorates the reefscape.

Tunicates: Spineless Chordates

One of the Caribbean's most common marine invertebrates, tunicates are often mistaken for sponges. Like the sponge, they usually have two siphons—one for drawing in nutrients and the other for expelling used water. Though some are free-swimming, most tunicates are attached to the reef at one end and come in a variety of often brilliant colors. Sometimes the tunicate is covered in algal growth, making it difficult to spot unless it is feeding and its siphon is open.

These creatures are difficult to photograph because they are light and pressure sensitive—when disturbed, muscular bands around the siphons rapidly contract. The common name "tunicate" comes from the animal's cellulose body covering, or "tunic." They are also commonly called sea squirts because some species, when irritated, will forcefully expel a stream of water from their excurrent opening. Tunicates may live singularly or in a colony, and sometimes a number of compound tunicates live together inside a common tunic with multiple incurrent siphons and a larger excurrent siphon.

Perhaps most unique about the tunicate is its seemingly unusual classification. Normally, chordates have backbones and are vertebrates. Not so with the tunicate. Classified as a urochordate, the tunicate has no backbone but is still included in the Chordata phylum. Why? At some point in the life cycle, all urochordates have a tail, a dorsal central nerve cord, pharyngael gill clefts and, at the larval stage, a notochord, which is a flexible, supportive rod made of cartilage. In vertebrates, the notochord is replaced by bone.

STEVE SIMONSEN

28 | Randy's Reef

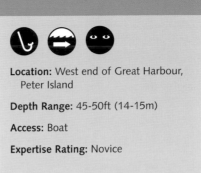

Because it's protected from all but the very worst weather, Randy's Reef is a good alternative site if poor conditions force you out of other sites. Unfortunately, visibility tends to be low—in the 20-to-30ft range—so don't be surprised.

If you are feeling the need for a tunicate fix, Randy's Reef is the place to go. The site's large coral heads are surrounded by many painted and bluebell tunicates. These tunicates grow as beautiful bundles of hundreds of small siphons, each measuring less than a half-inch long. The bodies are transparent, while the rim and tissue colors vary from light brown to deep purple. They are like flowers in a desert.

The site is also a good macro location. Look for little creatures such as nudibranchs, flatworms and feather dusters hiding inside the coral crevices. You may also find plenty of shrimp species, includ-

Location: West end of Great Harbour, Peter Island

Depth Range: 45-50ft (14-15m)

Access: Boat

Expertise Rating: Novice

ing banded coral shrimp, two-claw shrimp, peppermint shrimp and various cleaner shrimp.

Sharpnosed puffers prefer gorgonians and seagrass beds.

29 | *Rhone's* Anchor

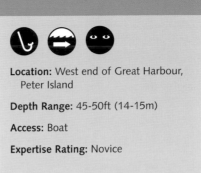

Over the last several hundred years, Great Harbor has hosted thousands of ships of all shapes and sizes. In exchange for the safe anchorage it provides, the harbor's vast coral floor has claimed small parts from its visitors by taking a firm grasp of many anchors and chains. Dozens of relics litter the bottom, but the most famous of these is the anchor that belonged to the RMS *Rhone.*

After many attempts at retrieving its anchor during a lull in the Hurricane of

Location: Great Harbour, Peter Island

Depth Range: 40-65ft (12-20m)

Access: Boat

Expertise Rating: Intermediate

1867, the *Rhone* had to cut it loose. The anchor is about 15ft long and lies half-engulfed by a large coral head. The other half hangs over a sandy bottom in about 70ft. A large chain extends away from the anchor.

The numerous other anchors of all sizes scattered throughout the area are a lasting reminder of the harbor's popularity in an era of great ships. Some of these lie close to that of the *Rhone*. *Rhone*'s Anchor is an official National Park site, so the removal of any and all artifacts—including old china and bottles you may see embedded in the coral—is prohibited.

Visibility in this area varies but can drop as low as 40ft. Throughout Great Harbour, large black-coral trees surround the coral heads, giving the area a surreal forested feel.

30 Truck Reef

Truck Reef is one of the BVI's deepest sites, with a mini-wall that drops down to the 100ft range. Huge black coral trees surround you as you approach the old vehicle dumping grounds, the result of a 1950s campaign to rid Tortola of unwanted vehicles in preparation for a visit from the British Queen Mother. A total of about six vehicles were tossed overboard. One suspects that the monarch hardly noticed their absence.

Over the years, the cars and jeeps have deteriorated into rubble, though some parts are still recognizable. The deterioration is always more pronounced after each passing storm. Large, bushy black-coral trees thrive here. You'll also find

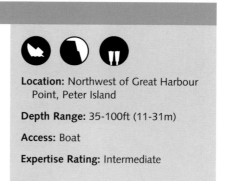

Location: Northwest of Great Harbour Point, Peter Island

Depth Range: 35-100ft (11-31m)

Access: Boat

Expertise Rating: Intermediate

dozens of old anchors left on the wall's edge by 18th- and 19th-century ships.

The site is unmarked and can be difficult to find. Divers will need a guide to pinpoint the site, which is just out of the harbor entrance, north of the *Fearless* buoy.

31 *Fearless & Willy T*

Two wrecks lie close together inside Peter Island's Great Harbour. The *Fearless*, a 110ft wooden minesweeper, was scuttled in 1986. At the time, it was rumored to be a sister ship to Cousteau's famous vessel *Calypso*, probably because of their similar wooden hulls. This legend continues, though no one is sure of its veracity. In 1995 the *Willy T*, a battered 90ft Baltic trader, was also put to rest nearby, just a short swim south of the *Fearless*. The *Willy T*

Location: West of Great Harbour Point, Peter Island

Depth Range: 30-85ft (9-26m)

Access: Boat

Expertise Rating: Intermediate

was the BVI's original floating restaurant and bar, but some serious wood damage ended her career in the catering business.

Visibility in Great Harbour is usually less than perfect, which in this case adds to the ghostly feel of the place. For your safety, it's best to circumnavigate the wrecks without actually penetrating them—their old age and brittle wooden bodies have seen better days and continue to decay.

Both wrecks are surrounded by black-coral trees and large, mature coral heads. Though fish life is varied, with large groupers appearing from time to time, this is not the ideal place for aquarium-type fish-watching.

Time has taken its toll on the *Fearless*'s wooden timbers.

32 Shark Point

Location: Just off Peter Island Bluff

Depth Range: 25-80ft (7.6-24m)

Access: Boat

Expertise Rating: Intermediate

Shark Point is a low-lying ridge that extends out from Peter Island's southeast peninsula. The ridge begins at about 60ft and slowly rises as it gets closer to shore. Here, large canyons, a rocky wall and a cul-de-sac cavern add excitement to an otherwise flat terrain.

Since it faces the Caribbean's southeast waters, Shark Point is exposed to pelagic life that comes in from the deeper waters. Sightings of manta rays are reported from time to time. True to the site's name, sharks are also seen occasionally—nurse or reef sharks are most common, but sometimes a lemon or bull shark cruises by.

The surface close to shore should not be overlooked, as this is where you'll find much of the fish activity. Schools of plankton-eating fish abound in the shallow surf.

Shark Point is not diveable most of the year due to strong easterly winds, swells and currents. When diveable, however, it is an exciting experience. In calm weather, the site's shallow rocks, canyons and passages are easily explored.

Dead Chest Island

Lying off Peter Island's northeast corner is Dead Chest, a small (less than a quarter-mile (.4km) wide) coffin-shaped island with more lore to it than one might expect. In the 19th-century heyday of pirating, a captain—possibly the infamous Blackbeard himself—marooned his mutinous crew here with only a barrel of rum and a goat. The stranded sailors tried desperately to swim across to Peter Island but drowned in the process, earning Deadman's Bay on Peter Island its morbid name.

Glassy sweepers occupy caves and caverns.

Today, Dead Chest Island lies quietly bathed by the waves of the Caribbean Sea and surrounded by beautiful shallow reefs to the north and rugged underwater canyons to the south.

It is a good idea to combine all the dives around Dead Chest into a day of diving. They are very different from one another, and since all the sites are relatively shallow, bottom time isn't much of an issue.

33 | Dead Chest West

This is an easy, protected dive site with lots of opportunities for macro and semi-wide-angle photography. The mild conditions and high visibility make Dead Chest West an excellent beginner's site, as well as a welcoming arena for the dedicated professional photographer.

Location: Southwest of Dead Chest Island

Depth Range: 15-55ft (4.6-17m)

Access: Boat

Expertise Rating: Novice

Two caves in the shallows attract glassy sweepers and silversides, but the best part of this dive is in and around the shallow coral gardens bordering the underwater cliffside on island's west side. You will find an abundance of tropical fish just about anywhere among the hard and soft corals, as well as in the sandy desert fields in the deeper water. Squid are common here, often camouflaging themselves among the gorgonians and soft-coral trees.

34 | Painted Walls

Three deep canyons carve their way into the island's south side. The canyon sides are covered with colorful sponges and soft corals—the site's "painted" walls. Unfortunately, many of the fabulous soft corals and sponges that earned the site its name were washed away during a series of storms that hit the islands in 1997. Luckily, much of the sessile life is gradually returning.

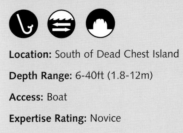

Location: South of Dead Chest Island

Depth Range: 6-40ft (1.8-12m)

Access: Boat

Expertise Rating: Novice

There's a lot to see in a small area—light plays off the site's many arches, cracks and crevices like a Grand Canyon sunset. Keep an eye out for octopuses and camouflaged frogfish. Squid patrol this area on a regular basis, and hawksbill turtles are often seen. Spend some time in the shallow surf above the canyons—you'll see schools of fish and hunting barracudas. Look for nurse sharks lazing under shallow coral heads.

A nurse shark sleeps between the site's "painted" walls.

35 Coral Gardens

At this site, small coral heads pile up into mushroom-shaped coral formations that reach toward the sun. Coral Gardens is a first-class snorkeling site. It is shallower than most BVI sites, so the coral life is vulnerable to storm damage. Although the reef changes every few years, it always manages to come back from even the most severe damage.

Location: North of Dead Chest Island

Depth Range: 15-35ft (4.6-11m)

Access: Boat

Expertise Rating: Novice

Hundreds of juvenile fish swim midwater among the coral formations, feeding in the current. Jacks, groupers and even larger fish stop by the many cleaning stations for a manicure by a spotfin hogfish or a scarlet-striped cleaner shrimp. Schools of blue tangs, southern sennets or yellow goatfish occupy every area. Watch for the occasional eagle ray or shark lurking along the reef.

Coral Gardens is even more spectacular at night. After dark, the coral blooms into a rich garden, and night critters come out in full force. Many types of lobster—including spiny, spotted, and slipper—play alongside red night shrimp and a variety of crabs.

A conservation-minded diver takes time out to participate in REEF's annual fish count.

Groomers of the Sea

Observant divers will find a variety of symbiotic relationships throughout the marine world—associations in which two dissimilar organisms participate in a mutually beneficial relationship. One of the most interesting relationships is found at cleaning stations, places where one animal (or symbiont) advertises its grooming services to potential clients with inviting, undulating movements.

Various species of cleaners—such as wrasse and shrimp—are dedicated to caring for their customers, which may include fish of all sizes and species. Larger fish such as sharks and mantas generally frequent cleaning stations that are serviced by angelfish, butterfly-fish and larger wrasse. Turtles usually seek out algae-feeding tangs that are eager to rid them of their algae buildup.

Customers hover in line until their turn comes. When the cleaner attends to a waiting customer—perhaps a grouper, parrotfish or even moray eel—it may enter the customer's mouth to perform dental hygiene, and even exit through the fish's gills. Although the customer could have an easy snack, it would never attempt to swallow the essential cleaner. The large fish benefits from the removal of parasites and dead tissue, while the little cleaner is provided with a meal.

Divers will find that if they carefully approach a cleaning station, they'll be able to get closer to many fish than is normally possible and observe behavior seen nowhere else on the reef.

STEVE ROSENBERG

A tiger grouper gets a cleaning from an eager pair of gobies.

Salt Island

Salt Island is named after the three salt pans within its shores. Before the age of refrigeration, a moderately sized population lived on the island and made their living harvesting and trading sea salt from the salt pans.

The tragic sinking of the RMS *Rhone* in 1867 put this small island on the worldwide map. The bravery of the islanders who assisted the wreck's survivors was rewarded by the British queen. In recognition of their service, islanders are to this day taxed only one bag of salt a year. The *Rhone* cemetery, with its shallow graves of coral stones, lies adjacent to the island settlement.

Today, only a handful of residents have survived the migration to the larger islands of Tortola and Virgin Gorda. A visit to the Salt Island settlement is well worth it—if you can find one of the residents, he or she will most likely be happy to sell you a pound of native salt, harvested and bagged as you watch.

36 | Blonde Rock

Blonde Rock is part of the shallow reef that the *Rhone* avoided in its scramble for open sea during a lull in the Hurricane of 1867. Of course, the unfortunate vessel hit Black Rock instead, sealing its fate.

Location: Salt Island Passage

Depth Range: 10-65ft (3-20m)

Access: Boat

Expertise Rating: Intermediate

Divers can explore a coral ledge riddled with caves, crevices and narrow holes. With all these handy places to hide, Blonde Rock could conceivably be renamed Lobster Heaven. Spiny and slipper lobsters, as well as all sorts of crabs and shrimp, emerge from hard-to-reach nooks and crannies. There is no lobstering allowed anywhere in the territory. Offenders will be fined by park rangers.

As you explore the underwater architecture, don't forget to look up at the schooling fish—including cobia and southern sennet (a small type of barracuda)—that like to congregate near the surface.

Schools of blackbar soldierfish and grunts mingle under ledges and overhangs at Blonde Rock.

37 *Rhone* **Reef**

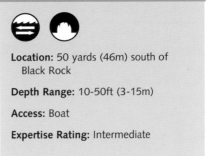

This site has all the signs of a tourist trap—a reef that lies close to a world-renowned shipwreck and borrows its name. But time and time again, *Rhone* Reef has proven itself to be one of the most beautiful spots anywhere in the BVI for macro and wide-angle photography.

Location: 50 yards (46m) south of Black Rock

Depth Range: 10-50ft (3-15m)

Access: Boat

Expertise Rating: Intermediate

The reef lies about 50 yards south of Salt Island's Black Rock, just south of the *Rhone*'s propeller. Literally hundreds of fish species congregate here in large numbers, including drums, highhats and glassy sweepers, to name just a few. Angelfish—including gray, queen and French varieties—are common here.

The site follows the rough contour of the island's southern geographical features and includes large boulders and bits of land broken off of the main island. Although the site leads into deeper water, many divers find the shallows to be the best. The bottom here varies from small pebbles and rocks to large pillar coral heads. As you enter the pebbled bottom field, look for the cavern to your left. The cavern is small, with enough room for one diver to enter, forcing the schools of sweepers outward in the process. The cavern may also house silversides and shrimp.

Conditions at the site are relatively calm, but the swim to and from the moorings over the stern section of the wreck can be strenuous, so go slowly.

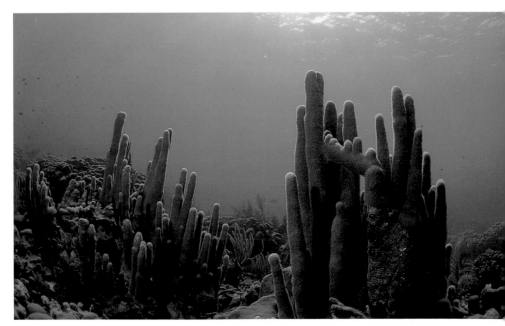

Distinctive pillar coral formations grow on many BVI reefs, offering protection to many fish species.

38 | RMS *Rhone*

Lying in three distinct sections (bow, midsection and stern) west of Salt Island, this 310ft twin-masted steamer is regarded as a classic among wreck dives. She sits in depths ranging from 20ft at the shallow stern section to 90ft at the deepest bow section.

The *Rhone* has always been the most popular dive site in the BVI. It also happens to be one of the most beautiful

38a Bow

Location: West side of Salt Island

Depth Range: 65-80ft (20-24m)

Access: Boat

Expertise Rating: Intermediate

38b Midsection

Location: West side of Salt Island

Depth Range: 50-70ft (15-21m)

Access: Boat

Expertise Rating: Intermediate

38c Stern

Location: West side of Salt Island, next to Black Rock Point

Depth Range: 20-50ft (6-15m)

Access: Boat

Expertise Rating: Novice

accessible backdrops in the world for wide-angle still and motion photography. In fact, the wreck was the primary filming location for the 1977 film *The Deep*, starring a youthful Nick Nolte and Jacqueline Bisset. The movie put the BVI on the worldwide diving map at a time when sport diving was in its infancy. Since then, the world-famous wreck has hosted hundreds of thousands of divers. This relentless exploration has not managed to diminish the grand old lady's unparalleled beauty.

Marine life around the wreck is abundant, and you'll see lots of hard and soft coral growth throughout the ship's structure. Even during a day dive, make sure to bring a good light, as there are lots of dark corners to light up in search of creatures. At night, the *Rhone* comes to life as the coral polyps open up to feed in the safety of darkness. Octopuses, eels, shrimp, rays and squid are common visitors and permanent residents. Other creatures that call the *Rhone* home include lobsters, several species of giant crab, scaly-tailed mantis shrimp and other crustaceans.

The site is understandably popular— to avoid diving traffic, try heading down in the early morning or late afternoon. Also, noon is often a very quiet time. You'll need to go on more than one dive to see the wreck in its entirety. It's best to visit the deeper bow section first, followed by the stern and midsection on a separate dive. Even these two dives are just a beginning—there is enough to see and explore that additional dives can only add to your experience.

The bow and midsection are for more advanced divers because of their

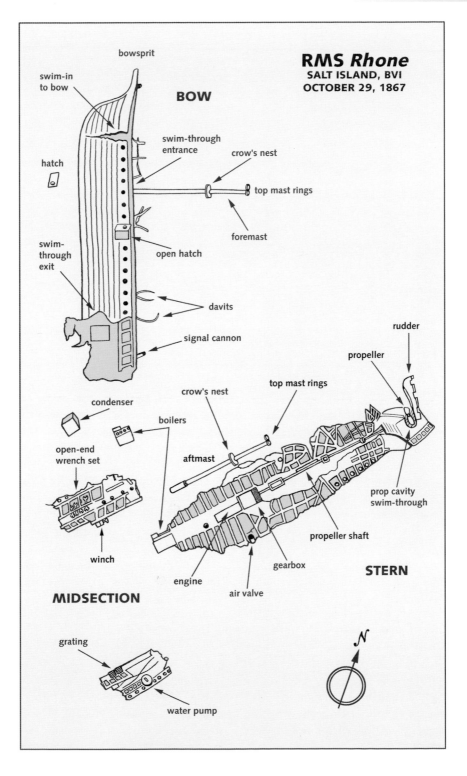

bowsprit

swim-in
to bow

BOW

RMS *Rhone*
SALT ISLAND, BVI
OCTOBER 29, 1867

swim-through
entrance

crow's nest

hatch

top mast rings

swim-
through
exit

foremast

open hatch

davits

signal cannon

rudder

propeller

crow's nest

top mast rings

condenser

boilers

open-end
wrench set

aftmast

prop cavity
swim-through

propeller shaft

winch

gearbox

engine

air valve

STERN

MIDSECTION

N

grating

water pump

One of the ship's signaling cannons lies pinned under the bow;
the other guards the entrance to Virgin Gorda's Bitter End Yacht Club.

depths, wreck-penetration possibilities and possible low visibility and current. During good weather conditions, however, dive operators will take promising novice divers here under direct instructor supervision. The less-challenging conditions at the shallow stern make it a novice site.

Visibility around the *Rhone* is usually excellent—about 60 to 100ft and better—but the occasional plankton bloom can drop visibility to as low as 40ft. On some days, the visibility can top 120ft and more. On these days, one can see the ship's entire bow section from tip to tip—an impressive sight indeed.

Occasionally, strong currents sweep the bow and midsection, though the stern is usually somewhat protected. Since these currents are usually wind-driven, they often affect only the first 20ft or so. Move quickly down the mooring line—but don't let go of the line—and you shouldn't have any problems.

Remember also that most of the ship is in relatively deep water, so your bottom time is limited. Don't attempt to cover the whole wreck in one go—approach the dive in sections. Local divers visit the wreck over and over again to get to know it intimately. You will want to schedule several dives to appreciate the ship's many charms.

RMS *Rhone* - Bow

The bow is the largest and most intact section of the wreck. This is the deepest section of the site and has been spared much of the battering of Mother Nature and Father Time—this part of the wreck has retained its original look and shows a variety of the ship's classic features.

The 150ft long bow section rests on its starboard side. The mast and crow's nest (lookout tower) are still attached to the ship. As the huge section broke away from the rest of the vessel, her interior opened for exploration. Exploring this portion is like entering a large, dimly lit cavern with a clear exit always visible. It's good to bring a reliable light for exploration of the interior. Many of the large beams are now completely exposed.

You'll see the ship's large bowsprit and the rigging that once hoisted the mast. Look for the large entrance hatch with its door wide open. The side of the ship is dotted with many portholes, many of them with polished brass and the glass still intact.

Farther aft, you can see the two main davits (cranes that held the lifeboats) resting on the seafloor. Closest to the break in the hull, you'll see additional columns and one of ship's two cannons, which is pinned beneath the bulk of the vessel. A short swim across the sand aft of the bow brings you to the condenser, which is honeycombed with holes that house lobsters and a particularly large green moral eel.

The mast and crow's nest are heavily encrusted with marine life.

The series of vertical deck beams is one of the most indelible images from the *Rhone* wreck site.

RMS *Rhone* - Midsection

In the *Rhone*'s midsection you'll see what appears to be a series of beautiful Greek columns. These are actually the support beams of the ship's deck, shorn of the teak boards and standing upright. The view of these columns on a clear day is almost mystical. One of the two boilers is here—it is large enough for divers to swim through.

Look for an oversized wrench set welded to the ship's steel framework. It is unclear whether the wrench set was fused to the ship's frame during the intense heat that proceeded the sinking, or if it was later bonded through coral growth.

Either way, the set is a permanent fixture here. The midsection structures are populated by many schools of fish, including horse-eyed jacks, grunts, spadefish and barracuda.

An additional south section lies somewhat removed from the rest of the wreck. Here you'll see more columns from the ship's main body, as well as the water pumps that failed to save her from sinking. The south section seems to attract larger schools of fish, especially during strong currents, when the schools hover in midwater feeding on plankton brought in by the current.

RMS *Rhone* - Stern

The stern is the shallowest section of the wreck. At some 150ft in length, it covers about the same area as the bow. The ship's oversized rudder lies beside the 15ft propeller, looking more or less as they would have when the ship was afloat. A swim through the coral-encrusted propeller housing is a highlight of this section. From here, the drive shaft (a large tube) traverses the gearbox, leading to one of the ship's two boilers. The stern mast lies alongside the remains. It was laid here to rest in the 1950s, after the British Navy considered the section a navigational hazard and subsequently opened the wreck further to sink it completely.

Over the years, divers have worked one of the bronze portholes into a high shine by rubbing it for good luck. It's easy to spot midway between the shaft support box and the mast's topside ring.

Snorkeling is outstanding in this shallow section. Yellowtail snappers and other midwater fish float about. Down on the bottom there are additional schools of grunts

The *Rhone*'s 15ft propeller is a highlight of the stern section.

and the like. Southern stingrays and eagle rays pass though here often.

History of the RMS *Rhone*

© NATIONAL MARITIME MUSEUM, LONDON

The Royal Mail Steamship *Rhone* was commissioned in Southampton, England, in 1865 by the Royal Mail Steam Packet Company. The ship's function was to transport mail, passengers and goods between England and its West Indian colonies and parts of South America. She measured in at 310ft (95m) in length with a 40ft (12m) beam.

The *Rhone* was a fine ship, ahead of her time and in a category all to herself. While other ships of her day were still paddle-driven, the *Rhone* was a full sailing twin-masted schooner with the additional ability to sail under power, using her huge steam engine and large single propeller. The vessel could navigate foul weather, traveling at a comfortable pace of 14 knots (17mph or 27km/h.)

In 1867 she anchored in Peter Island's Great Harbour, across from Tortola's main port at Road Town. She had been relocated here because of a yellow-fever epidemic in St. Thomas, her normal port of call. On October 29 she lay on Great Harbour alongside a paddleship named the *Conway*. When the weather began to deteriorate, the two experienced ship captains assured one another that hurricane season had already passed and incorrectly expected a mild northerly storm. If the captains had known a hurricane was coming, they probably would have set sail for open seas. A ship of the *Rhone*'s size would have been much safer in open water under hurricane conditions.

As the storm worsened, the ships were knocked about by northern winds and waves. During a lull in the storm later that day, the captains again consulted and decided to set out for open waters. The lull they experienced was in fact the eye of a large hurricane, which would go on to batter the islands, this time from the south. This was another unfortunate decision, as the *Rhone* would have been safer where she was, protected from the south by the hills on Peter Island.

History of the RMS *Rhone*

The *Rhone*'s 3,000lb (1,350kg) anchor and 300ft (92m) of chain had become embedded in a coral head and had to be cut loose. Without tackle, the ship had no option but to leave for open water. It left the harbor and headed out past Salt Island, giving wide berth to the underwater hazard of Blonde Rock. When the second part of the storm hit, the *Rhone* was powering full steam ahead toward the southern Caribbean Sea.

The ship's steam engines were no match for the powerful storm—the ship was eventually blown backward onto Salt Island's Black Rock. A large gash in her hull drew in cold water, which struck the extremely hot and overworked boilers. The ensuing explosion ripped the ship in half. The stern sank immediately, while the bow swung around and slid down to its current position. The force of the storm was such that if the vessel had been thrown to one or the other side of the rock, it may have actually ended up on a sandy shore. There were only a half-dozen survivors—five crew members and a single passenger.

The residents of Salt Island did all they could to help the injured and bury the dead. In recognition of their brave efforts during the terrible ordeal, the queen of England granted them ownership of the small salt-producing island for life. Their yearly taxation, still collected to this day, is a single bag of salt.

In the years after the sinking, hard-hat divers recovered much of the cargo. Even as late as the 1970s and '80s, full sets of china and other beautiful pieces emerged in private collections. Today the site is protected by the BVI's National Park Trust. All artifacts found must remain underwater for others to enjoy.

There is no memorial in the BVI for the *Rhone*. A small, simple history museum on Main Street in Road Town displays artifacts and some large blueprints of the ship. In an overgrown cemetery in Southampton, England, however, there is a beautiful commemorative monument honoring those that perished so far from home on that fateful day. It is the only known memorial to the *Rhone*.

The *Rhone* memorial lies in an overgrown cemetery in Southhampton, England.

Southeast Dive Sites

The southeast section covers a large area and includes sites around Cooper Island, Ginger Island and their adjacent rocks. The sites tend to be relatively close together.

Cooper Island has a filling station and satellite dive shop operated by Underwater Safaris, a dive operator based out of Road Town. Cooper is a convenient base for exploring the southeast area. Many of the southeast dive sites are exposed to current and to the open waters of the Caribbean Sea to the south. Stormy seas or extremely high winds can limit diving in this area. Some of the sites are rather remote, lending a sensation of isolation. Visibility is usually very high in these waters.

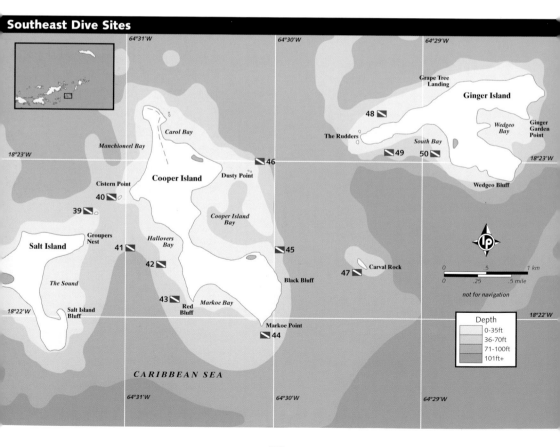

Southeast Dive Sites

Local fisherfolk hang their nets out to dry on Cooper Island's shores.

Southeast Dive Sites

	Good Snorkeling	Novice	Intermediate	Advanced
39 Vanishing Rock	●	●		
40 Cistern Point	●	●		
41 *Inganess Bay*				●
42 *Marie L & Pat*				●
43 Thumb Rock	●		●	
44 Markoe Point	●		●	
45 Devil's Kitchen			●	
46 Dry Rocks East	●		●	
47 Carval Rock	●		●	
48 Alice's Backstep	●		●	
49 Alice in Wonderland			●	
50 Ginger Steps			●	

Cooper Island

Cooper Island is perhaps the main social gathering spot in this area. Sailors often stop over before continuing on to the BVI's northern islands. Although it is a very popular anchorage, at times it can be an uncomfortable stay because of the swells that creep into the bay.

Cooper is a great place to take a break. There is one main beach, no road and all the goats you could wish for. The main onshore attraction is the Cooper Island Beach Club, the island's only restaurant and bar (and not really a club at all). It's a pleasant place to rest between dives or pass the time while you wait for tanks to be refilled. The meals are large and tasty, and the owners recently added some small lodgings.

39 | Vanishing Rock

What distinguishes Vanishing Rock is its location in the middle of a narrow passage. Fish are attracted to the site from nearby Salt and Cooper Islands and enjoy the area's expansive coral gardens. Vanishing Rock dips quickly from the surface to a shallow bottom at about 40ft. The rock is visible above the surface in even the calmest weather.

Since the current here usually runs east to west, the west side tends to be the calmest to dive. The current is usually mild enough that you can circumnavi-

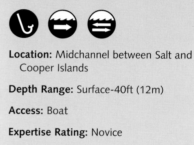

Location: Midchannel between Salt and Cooper Islands

Depth Range: Surface-40ft (12m)

Access: Boat

Expertise Rating: Novice

gate the rock, exploring its many nooks, crannies and overhangs. Pockets of fish congregate, especially near the surface.

A golden moray warily surveys its surroundings from its hiding place.

Sergeant majors often hover inside the cut that separates the main rock from a smaller one next to it. Look for sleeping nurse sharks under the overhangs. Sea fans, gorgonians and other underwater "trees" decorate the bottom.

40 Cistern Point

Cistern Point is a great snorkeling site, with a lot happening just below the surface. A few small underwater canyons cut across the rocky bottom, hosting a variety of fish. Although the busy overnight anchorage at Manchioneel Bay attracts many snorkelers to this site, it never gets truly overcrowded. Cistern Point is a good novice dive site as well.

When the seas pound the coastline, the surf builds and breaks around this small peninsula. Divers sometimes encounter reef sharks at Cistern Point, usually close to shore in the breaking surf. Small sharks

Location: Just south of Manchioneel Bay, Cooper Island

Depth Range: Surface-30ft (9.1m)

Access: Boat

Expertise Rating: Novice

take advantage of the low visibility to hunt for their prey. The sharks are unlikely to pose a threat to divers—they usually dart out of the way and disappear.

41 *Inganess Bay*

The *Inganess Bay*, a 150ft freighter, was sunk by the BVI Dive Association as part of an ongoing artificial reef project. The *Inganess Bay* is the longest and largest of all the scuttled vessels in the BVI. The wreck lies completely upright on a sandy bottom with no adjacent reefs. It sits in the middle of the channel that runs between Salt and Cooper Islands.

Permanent marine life has not yet taken to the wreck. Though some fish visit, and pelagics pass by occasionally, the huge schools that were expected to take refuge in the wreck have not yet arrived. It is possible that the area's

Location: Midchannel between Salt and Cooper Islands

Depth Range: 45-80ft (14-24m)

Access: Boat

Expertise Rating: Advanced

The ship's propeller is not obscured by invertebrate growth.

moderate currents have slowed the invertebrate growth necessary to attract a large fish population. Most divers expect that it is merely a matter of time before fish begin to populate the wreck.

In the meantime, the wreck retains an intriguing larger-than-life feel. There is some current, so the water tends to be very clear. The clarity of the water combines with the structure's isolated location to create a surreal effect—it looks like the ship is steaming full-speed ahead through a sea of sand. The vessel has a towering bridge in the rear, and its long, large cargo bay stretches toward the bow.

Lying upright, the tanker seems to sail along a sea of sand.

42 Marie L & Pat

OK, the intention was never to place one wreck almost on top of another—the good people from the BVI Dive Association slightly missed their intended mark, and this site is the result. The wrecks of the *Marie L* and the *Pat* now seem inseparable and complement each other nicely.

The *Marie L*, a 75ft interisland cargo vessel, was intentionally sunk in 1990 to add dimension to an already popular reef site. She lies in about 85ft on a sandy bottom, about 75ft from a large healthy reef. The remains of the *Pat*, a 90ft freighter, were scuttled here in 1995. The two vessels lie next to each other, bow to stern, with only a few feet separating the two. (The *Marie L* is the vessel that is closer to the reef.) Both vessels sank upright, affording divers an interesting perspective.

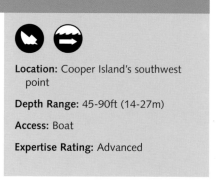

Location: Cooper Island's southwest point

Depth Range: 45-90ft (14-27m)

Access: Boat

Expertise Rating: Advanced

The wrecks have already attracted much marine life to their empty steel hulls. Groupers, a small jewfish, French angelfish and a few schools of grunts have taken up residence in the deckhouses and cargo bays, which are clear of debris and safe to enter. The relatively deep sandy bottom is full of life and hosts a large colony of garden eels. Southern stingrays, eagle rays and small sharks patrol this area. On the reef, groups of iridescent blue chromis are everywhere. Visibility here usually exceeds 100ft.

Double your pleasure with these two wrecks that lie one next to the other.

43 Thumb Rock

Something unusual happens at this site—the visibility and water color change dramatically within just a few yards. The Thumb Rock dive site follows the contours of Cooper's Red Bluff Point. The visibility, which is compromised near shore, improves markedly as you get away from the shoreline. The lower nearshore visibility isn't due to runoff—it's just the way the water flows around the point.

Follow the shoreline, keeping the rock face to your left. This brings you to a left-hand bend, which leads to an open underwater field. It is here that the visibility improves. The rock-and-coral bottom is dotted with soft-coral trees. Many common Caribbean fish species are present here, but the site's

Location: Southwest of Red Bluff Point

Depth Range: 20-60ft (6-18m)

Access: Boat

Expertise Rating: Intermediate

main attraction is the large number of tarpon.

The site's unusual visibility pattern may offer some advantage in the tarpon's hunting patterns, which would explain why these predators typically gather here. The tarpon's large silver body and upturned lower jaw are unmistakable. The experience is even more impressive when large balls of silversides—tarpon's main source of food—are present. The tarpon feed through the schools, forcing the tiny fish to flee and transforming the cloud of fish into unusual shapes. Even if you happen upon a quiet day, be patient—a few tarpon will make an appearance.

Tarpon Tales

Tarpon (*Megalops atlanticus*) are long silvery fish distinguished by their upturned mouths. Because of their size—up to 7ft (2.1m) in length, but more often 2 to 4ft (.6 to 1.2m) long—and their upright dorsal fins, divers sometimes mistake tarpon for sharks. Tarpon are renowned game fish, known for their tremendous fighting ability when hooked. Luckily

for them, tarpon meat is definitely not worth tasting.

A female tarpon lays some 13 million eggs in a single spawn, but very few of these eggs survive to maturity. During the day, you will often see tarpon in large schools, swimming slowly around reefs, seagrass areas, canals and other secluded spots. At night they hunt either alone or in pairs, working in tandem to attack small schools of fish.

—*Reef Line*, the newsletter of Reef Relief

44 | Markoe Point

Markoe Point is Cooper Island's southernmost outcropping, reaching toward the open waters of the Caribbean Sea. Like the cliffside above the water, the site's bottom contours are rough. The rocks are riddled with great gashes where fish hide from predators.

It is a visually pleasing site, both above and below. Markoe Point is somewhat removed from evidence of human development, giving the area an isolated feel. At the site's southernmost point, a large rock climbs straight up from the bottom like a large, thick needle. Lean over the top of this needle

Location: Off Markoe Point

Depth Range: 30-60ft (9.1-18m)

Access: Boat

Expertise Rating: Intermediate

and pretend to be a skydiver leaping out into the void—the feeling is exhilarating.

Divers visit Markoe Point more for its geological interest than for fishwatching. That said, you'll see plenty of typical reef fish, as well as barracuda, jacks, permit, pompano and other open-water species that come in for inspection. Most are just passing by in search of food.

The surface can be rough. Currents are common—be sure to start your dive against the current, so you can drift back with it. If you drift too far offshore here, your next stop could be Florida.

Markoe Point's pinnacle is a dramatic example of the area's underwater topography.

45 Devil's Kitchen

Devil's Kitchen is very different from other reef dives in the area. The mooring is in about 15ft over a shallow coral bottom. A small drop-off east of the mooring leads to a sandy bottom, which is really the beginning of the dive.

At 40ft a long overhang of about 600ft opens up. Underneath this protective mantle, large gatherings of smallmouth and Caesar grunts mingle peacefully, interrupted by the occasional burst of a hungry barracuda, jack or shark. Smallmouth grunts are blue or silver, with yellow fins and five or six narrow yellow stripes running the length of their

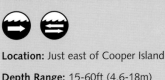

Location: Just east of Cooper Island

Depth Range: 15-60ft (4.6-18m)

Access: Boat

Expertise Rating: Intermediate

bodies. Caesar grunts are similar in color, but with dusky blue fins and much narrower yellow stripes.

Look for spotted lobsters, which are common in the BVI. Also, Devil's Kitchen hosts what may be the most diverse snapper population in the territory: look for mutton snappers, dog snappers and schoolmasters. You can also see fairy basslets hanging upside-down under the ledges—their purple-and-gold bodies are striking and unmistakable.

Devil's Kitchen is a safe dive under most conditions, but currents here can be strong. Also, be cautious during your entrance and exit—the mooring is close to the shallow reef, so it can be dangerous when swells kick in.

A mutton hamlet rests on the sandy bottom.

46 Dry Rocks East

This isolated shallow ridge east of Cooper Island breaks the surface in all weather. The main rock has a split near the top that forms a shallow channel. This is the only way to cross from one side of the ridge to the other without circumnavigating the entire formation. The ridge slopes gently to a rocky bottom. There are no large coral formations on the ridge itself, maybe because the rock is quite exposed. As you venture deeper, however, corals are plentiful, with both soft and hard species present. Isolated boulders dot the area just north of the ridge's underwater skirt.

Wind and occasional currents create a strong surge, which in turn attracts thousands of sergeant majors, as well as large schools of pelagic species such as barracuda, jacks, permit, schooling spadefish and other plankton-eaters. The fish activity is best appreciated from near the breaking surf close to the surface. You should, however, stay below the surface surge and watch your buoyancy to avoid rising too fast or rubbing

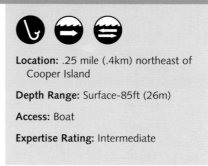

Location: .25 mile (.4km) northeast of Cooper Island

Depth Range: Surface-85ft (26m)

Access: Boat

Expertise Rating: Intermediate

against the fire coral that blankets the rocks.

At the site's deeper sections, coral and rocky boulders abound, providing shelter for many species of fish. Dry Rocks East is an open-water site, so surface and underwater currents keep visibility high—in the 70-to-100ft range. Strong currents and surge are always possible here, so beware.

Most of the site's marine-life activity happens on the northeast side of the rocks. In calm weather you can circumnavigate the rocks through the shallow water, allowing you an exciting, up-close view of the hunting activity.

Sergeant majors and other fish enjoy the exposed conditions of Dry Rocks East.

47 Carval Rock

Carval Rock is a large and especially isolated rock that runs north to south. The rock is as rugged underwater as it is above water. Nearby, other large boulders and small shelves break the waves. It is exposed to weather from both the east and the south, making diving here difficult or impossible for most of the year. The best time to dive Carval Rock is in the summer or during the calm weather between lows or cold fronts, when the seas flatten and the wind dies down.

Weather permitting, Carval Rock can be an exciting departure from the more commonly visited sites in the area. Channels of sand on the seafloor are bordered by both soft and hard corals. As at other sites, lots of small tropical fish hide among the formations. Schools of fish hide in the surf, as jacks and other pelagics hunt just beneath the surface.

Location: Ginger Island Passage, west of Cooper Island

Depth Range: 15-90ft (4.6-27m)

Access: Boat

Expertise Rating: Intermediate

Barracuda are commonly seen here. Small caves and caverns shelter fishes of all types, including large pufferfish. Pufferfish inflate only when stressed—divers should enjoy watching the fish without harassing them.

Carval Rock's main activity is in the shallow waters close to the rocks, where you can see the waves breaking above you like thunderclouds. In heavy seas, however, the waves break strongly here, so be cautious.

Ginger Island

Ginger Island is a dramatic piece of uninhabited real estate east of Cooper Island.

It has sheer cliffs on its north and south sides and a perfect cove to the east. Some of the territory's best coral formations lie just off Ginger Island in depths of 40 to 75ft. The dramatic topography of Ginger Island is best experienced from the air, where you can see the cliffs' steep drops and the reef lagoon to the south.

Rugged Ginger Island offers cliffs and a gorgeous lagoon.

48 | Alice's Backstep

The north coast of Ginger Island is full of traditional coral formations, with all the variety expected from a healthy reef. Sponges are the main attraction here. You'll see sponges of all colors, shapes and forms—pretty much every type in

Location: North of Ginger Island's western tip

Depth Range: 20-70ft (6-21m)

Access: Boat

Expertise Rating: Intermediate

the book. If you have a sponge fetish that needs appeasing, this is the place. Don't forget to look inside the sponges for small critters—including little crab, shrimp and gobies—that call these ocean filters home.

Since there's a lot of ground to cover at this site and there tends to be a current here, a drift dive works as a natural approach. The easterly currents are not usually strong, but are just enough to push you along.

A lizardfish camouflaged against the sand.

49 Alice in Wonderland

Alice in Wonderland offers some of the best deepwater coral reefs in the BVI. The formations are large, striking and very healthy. Because of the reefs' depth and location, they have largely escaped the hurricane damage seen at other sites. Coral bleaching—in which corals are killed by abnormally high water temperatures—has also had less impact in this area than elsewhere.

A large spur-and-groove reef covers the bottom. Staghorn corals pile up in layers, turning the seascape into a surreal storybook land of 15ft mushroom-shaped formations, lending the site its name. The strips of towering corals are separated by narrow sand grooves, which lead to an even deeper sandy field.

The site's healthy grouper population attracts apex predators such as blacktip sharks, reef sharks and barracuda. Pockets of schooling fish—including grunts,

Location: South of Ginger Island's western tip

Depth Range: 40-80ft (12-24m)

Access: Boat

Expertise Rating: Intermediate

soldierfish and angelfish—lurk in the grooves and underneath the soft corals.

The reef's deeper section is a sea of sand. Spotted eagle rays—look for their white spots and pale underbodies—cruise the sand in search of mollusks. Southern stingrays also hunt along the sandy expanse. Meanwhile, large colonies of garden eels dance in the current.

Because the site is exposed to wind and weather, not all dive operators come here, and certainly not on a daily basis. Though night dives here would be amazing, the site's distance from a safe harbor tends to keep independent divers away.

50 Ginger Steps

Ginger Steps is one of the area's deepest coral dives. Crab, shrimp and schools of fish abound on ledges and overhangs and in small crevices, which spill rapidly to a bottom of powdery white sand. Though Ginger Steps lies just west of Alice in Wonderland and they share much of the same marine life, its coral formations are much smaller.

Ginger Steps lies close to the open water, making it an ideal arena for encounters with larger pelagics. Eagle rays, southern stingrays and the occasional manta ray make appearances, as do reef sharks and barracuda. Green, spotted and golden morays hide inside countless miniature tunnels and secret passage-

Location: Southwest of Ginger Island

Depth Range: 40-100ft (12-31m)

Access: Boat

Expertise Rating: Intermediate

ways. These are night feeders that seldom venture out during the day. The desert sea is alive with marine life—garden eels, flounders, mantis shrimp and other burrowing creatures occupy the sandy areas.

This is one of the deepest sites in the BVI, so take care not to exceed bottom times. Visibility is always excellent.

Northeast Dive Sites

The second-largest populated island in the BVI and a haven for both sailors and nature lovers, Virgin Gorda lies about 5 miles (8km) east of Tortola. It is home to The Baths, one the territory's best-known snorkeling and daytrip spots, where visitors explore the turquoise waters around and between a number of house-sized boulders.

Midway between Tortola and Virgin Gorda lie the Dog Islands, a group of isolated cays that offer unique diving opportunities. The Dogs also offer protection for sailors, making the area a favorite for isolated anchorage. A number of popular dive sites lie around the islands, while a few other sites are scattered farther offshore. Conditions in this area tend to be rougher during the winter, as most sites are exposed to north swells.

Northeast dive sites are more accessible to operators from Virgin Gorda than those on Tortola.

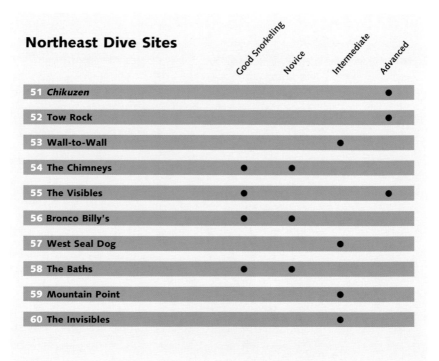

Northeast Dive Sites	Good Snorkeling	Novice	Intermediate	Advanced
51 *Chikuzen*				●
52 **Tow Rock**				●
53 **Wall-to-Wall**			●	
54 **The Chimneys**	●	●		
55 **The Visibles**	●			●
56 **Bronco Billy's**	●	●		
57 **West Seal Dog**			●	
58 **The Baths**	●	●		
59 **Mountain Point**			●	
60 **The Invisibles**			●	

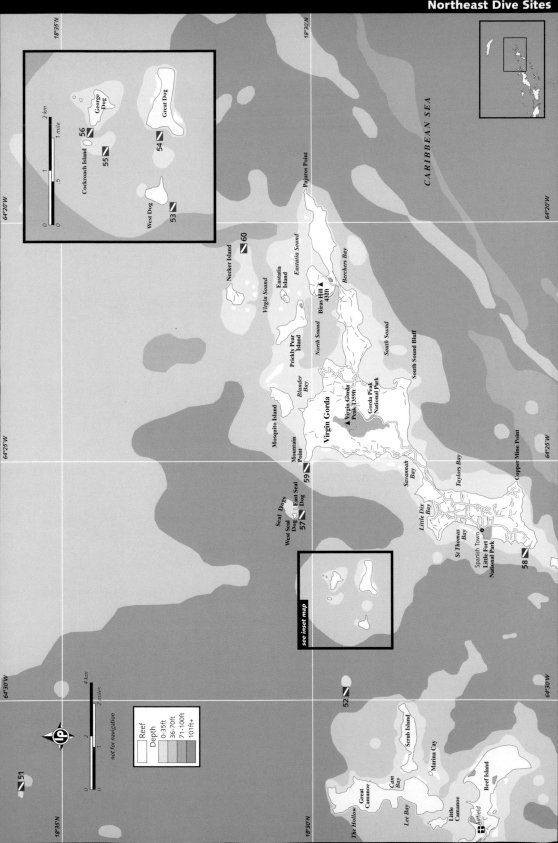

CARIBBEAN SEA

George Dog
Great Dog
Cockroach Island
56
55
54
West Dog
53
2 km
1 mile
.5
1
0
0

Pajaros Point

Necker Island
60

Virgin Sound
Eustatia Sound
Eustatia Island

Berchers Bay
Biras Hill
431ft

Prickly Pear Island
North Sound

South Sound
South Sound Bluff

Mosquito Island
Blunder Bay

Virgin Gorda
Virgin Gorda Peak 1359ft
Gorda Peak National Park

Mountain Point
59

Seal Dogs
West Seal Dog
East Seal Dog
57
57

Savannah Bay

Taylors Bay
Copper Mine Point

Little Dix Bay

St Thomas Bay
Spanish Town
Little Fort National Park
58

see inset map

52

Reef
Depth
0-35ft
36-70ft
71-100ft
101ft+

not for navigation

4 km
2 miles
2
0
1

LP

51

The Hollow
Great Camanoe
Lee Bay
Cam Bay
Marina Cay
Scrub Island
Little Camanoe
Beef Island
Airfield

Dog Islands

West of Virgin Gorda, the Dog Islands consist of five principal islands and a handful of smaller rocks. All are uninhabited. Visitors come to the island group to experience the many secluded anchorages and isolated diving and snorkeling spots. There are a few beaches, but the inland terrain is generally inhospitable—the waters around the islands are the area's most attractive feature by far.

51 | *Chikuzen*

The 246ft *Chikuzen* was shrouded in mystery the moment it entered BVI waters in 1981, burning and drifting aimlessly off Tortola's east coast. It seemed that the vessel had been abandoned by its crew and left to drift ablaze. When a local tugboat intervened to divert the ship from running aground, the tug's towline snapped, seriously injuring a crewmember. No one knew where the vessel had come from or who would bear responsibility for it. The *Chikuzen* was left to sink in 80ft of open water more than 5 miles north of Great Camanoe Island.

Location: 5.5 miles (9km) north of Great Camanoe Island

Depth Range: 45-80ft (14-24m)

Access: Boat

Expertise Rating: Advanced

Found mostly in deep waters, Atlantic spadefish school for protection.

The ship's history eventually came to light. In preparation for an incoming hurricane, the harbormaster on St. Martin—a French and Dutch island some 90 miles east of the BVI—requested that an unnamed refrigeration ship be moved to open waters. The poorly maintained ship was part of a Japanese fishing fleet based on St. Martin. Rather than take her to sea, the ship's owner quietly set the aging vessel on fire and allowed her to drift away, probably hoping to rid himself of his decrepit burden. Rather than sink as expected, the ship drifted westward into BVI waters.

Today the *Chikuzen* lies on a barren sandy bottom, attracting large pelagics to her empty carcass. She lies on her port side, and her rails come to within 45ft of the surface. The vessel's large railings, winches, halyards and propeller remain intact and are clearly visible in the site's clear waters. The *Chikuzen* is probably the most abundant wreck site in the BVI in terms of marine life. Large balls of fish, including grunts and jacks, congregate inside and around her steel hull. Barracuda cruise above the wreck in midwater. Cobias, squadrons of eagle rays, 300lb jewfish, sharks and other large pelagics come in for a close look at this underwater desert oasis.

Operators do not visit the wreck regularly, as weather and other conditions often prevent dive boats from safely venturing this far from the islands. Because of the distance, it also tends to be a bit more expensive to get to this site. The experience is usually well worth the cost. Night dives here are simply unforgettable under a full moon—the sandy bottom reflects the moonlight, bathing the wreck in an eerie soft light.

52 Tow Rock

About a mile west of West Dog Island, Tow Rock is an especially difficult site to find—it is completely submerged and has no marker or mooring to distinguish it from the area's open waters. Surrounded by jagged edges and overhangs, this underwater pinnacle rises to about 12ft from the surface. Tow Rock is one of the premier spots in the territory to see large schools of fish.

Hundreds and sometimes thousands of schooling fish gather around the rock to escape the area's strong current. As many as a dozen barracuda eagerly await their prey, while schooling fish—including French grunts, jacks and palometa—huddle around the rocks. Closer to the bottom, hordes of lobsters scuttle about.

Location: West of West Dog Island

Depth Range: 12-60ft (3.6-18m)

Access: Boat

Expertise Rating: Advanced

Dive operators don't travel to Tow Rock. In fact, many guides have never visited here at all. If you want to visit, you'll have to request it specially and insist that you have heard it's worth the trip. Because of the strong currents and low visibility, Tow Rock is only appropriate for experienced divers, and you should only visit this site with an experienced guide or skipper.

For divers, barracuda are less menacing than they appear.

53 Wall-to-Wall

Wall-to-Wall is what is known as a fifty-fifty dive site, which describes the likelihood of encountering the site packed wall-to-wall with schooling fish. After entering the water at West Dog's southwest wall, keep the land to your right and follow the island's skirt into deeper water. As you round the corner, you'll enter the area that, if you're lucky, will be packed with fish.

Ledges, overhangs and healthy corals dominate the landscape. The main attraction is the site's southwest corner, where schools of French grunts, schoolmasters, porkfish, squirrelfish and bigeyes often gather. Wall-to-Wall is one of the few places in the territory to see the cottonwick, a beautiful member of the grunt family. The cottonwick is distinguished

Location: Southwest of West Dog Island

Depth Range: 15-65ft (4.6-20m)

Access: Boat

Expertise Rating: Intermediate

from other grunts by bold black markings on its snout, dorsal fin and tail.

The site is accessible for most divers. It is protected from most easterly winds and northern swells. Currents sometimes kick up but are rarely a problem. North swells cause concern when they get large enough to creep around the southwest side, increasing surge at the site.

54 The Chimneys

Although this is one of the BVI's most visited sites, its beauty and excitement remain intact. Below the mooring you'll find an area that is affectionately known as "The Fishbowl," as most of the BVI's fish species are present. Calm and relatively shallow, The Chimneys is an understandable favorite of snorkelers and novice divers.

Location: West of Great Dog Island

Depth Range: 15-45ft (4.6-14m)

Access: Boat

Expertise Rating: Novice

The site's "chimneys"—an archway and a few big tunnels—lie north of the mooring. The principal archway is about 25ft wide and leads to a smaller crack in the bedrock. Wide enough for a diver to pass through, this crack leads to a large canyon.

The topography is diver-friendly—the top is never completely enclosed, and you'll always have a way up. Soft white sponges cover the walls of the geological formations. This sessile life hosts crabs, shrimp, lobsters and other small crustaceans.

In addition to exploring the canyons, archways, crevices and large overhangs, you'll find plenty of marine life to watch. Keep an eye out for apex predators such as barracuda, who skulk by in search of prey.

This small crack is one of the few entrances to The Chimneys.

55 The Visibles

The Visibles is a small underwater sea-mount just off Cockroach Island in the north section of the Dog Islands. It is known for its usually strong current and its many schools of fish, as well as some pelagic action. The Visibles can be a dull dive if you're caught in zero-current conditions—in this case, the visibility drops and even the fish disappear. Most days, however, the swift currents make this attractive for advanced divers—so jump in and hang on. Don't try to swim too far—you can find protection in the lee of the pinnacle.

South of the pinnacle lies a field of healthy gorgonians and large sea fans. Porcupinefish, cowfish, filefish, trunkfish and triggerfish lay low in the protection of this thick forest. You'll see moray eels and octopuses. Turtles swim near the bottom between the soft corals—hawksbill are the most common. It's not unusual to see a passing eagle ray or shark.

Location: Off Cockroach Island

Depth Range: 10-80ft (3-24m)

Access: Boat

Expertise Rating: Advanced

The best action lies north of the pinnacle in the deeper waters. Since the current usually runs south, you'll have to swim against the current a little to get here. Once you reach the north side of the pinnacle, the site drops off to deeper water. Here, 6ft-tall deepwater gorgonians await you in 60-to-80ft waters. Schools of bigeye are everywhere, and the occasional lemon shark comes in for a look.

In calm weather conditions, there is great snorkeling around the pinnacle and around nearby Cockroach Island.

A filefish swims in a current-swept gorgonian field at The Visibles.

Underwater treats await you on the other side of the archway leading to Bronco Billy's.

56 Bronco Billy's

Jacques Cousteau himself named this site, during the years he was running a summer program for kids on Mosquito Island, just north of Virgin Gorda. Bronco Billy's was known to be one of his favorite dive spots in the BVI.

Location: Off George Dog's western tip

Depth Range: 10-50ft (3-15m)

Access: Boat

Expertise Rating: Novice

Here, high arches and deep, cutting canyons filled with fish and healthy corals create a maze for exploration. On the site's north side, two deep, wide canyons are carved into George Dog. The canyon bottoms are not composed of coral, but rather of small polished stones like those you'd find in a freshwater river.

The site is usually filled with fish of all shapes and sizes—probably one of the reasons Cousteau loved it. At times, large schools of Caribbean reef squid patrol the archway that marks the site's entrance. As they move, the squid quickly change color to blend in with their surroundings.

Bronco Billy's faces north and is therefore susceptible to strong swells. Currents can also play a large part as water flows around the islands. Although usually very high, visibility can deteriorate rapidly to less than 30ft when there is a plankton bloom.

57 West Seal Dog

The Seal Dogs—West and East—are the northernmost islands in the Sir Francis Drake Channel, before it intersects with the Atlantic. They rise gently from the surrounding shallows and are completely deserted. The two islands sit close together, separated by a strip of shallow water. Since West Seal Dog is small, it can be affected by north swells and strong currents.

Location: Southwest corner of West Seal Dog

Depth Range: 15-70ft (4.6-21m)

Access: Boat

Expertise Rating: Intermediate

Although both islands are diveable, West Seal Dog is the more popular of the pair. Underwater, a few large coral and rock formations are scattered on the bottom. The fish population is large, with both reef and pelagic species present. Divers will see the usual array of fish, including schooling grunts, groupers and oldwives (the local name for queen triggerfish). The area's healthy corals include pillar and brain corals. Take time to explore the area's fabulous macro life, but don't forget to watch for pelagics that zoom in from the deep. Because of the island's northern location, close to the Atlantic, divers in the winter months are likely to hear humpbacks singing.

Grunts school in the lee of a large boulder to escape the area's swift current.

Virgin Gorda

The island of Virgin Gorda is known as much for its swank accommodations as for its natural attractions. With a population of about 2,000, Virgin Gorda's pace is slower than Tortola's—goats frequently take over the road. Sheltered on all sides, the Gorda Sound is like a huge saltwater lake. Though the wind blows through constantly, waves are low. and the water is clear.

The island's mountainous interior is protected as the Gorda Peak National Park—its highest point reaches 1,389ft (417m). Visitors can explore ancient copper mines, as well as many isolated pristine beaches accessible only by boat.

Diving is mostly limited to a few good spots off the island's protected west coast. There are a few isolated reefs to the north, which can be explored only under the calmest conditions. Dive operators based on Virgin Gorda tend to travel to the Dog Islands for most of their regular diving.

58 The Baths

Though The Baths is not a true dive site, it has a lot to offer the novice diver in particular. The site has achieved world-class stature because of its unmatched natural beauty—it is considered one of the best snorkeling sites in the BVI.

The "baths" are shallow pools of water between large granite boulders. The boulders are characteristic of Virgin Gorda's entire southern peninsula. Shallow crevices and small caverns attract fish, which come in from the surrounding sandy-bottomed areas. You won't find many fish in the pools, but there are plenty if you venture out beyond the boulders on the ocean side.

Keep an eye out for the rare chain moray. About 2ft long, this beautiful eel is dark brown with bright-yellow line patterns—it looks like it is wrapped with a gold chain. The Baths should be explored on land as well as from the water. If you climb up onto the boulders, you get a great view of the surrounding shallow waters with their few isolated coral heads.

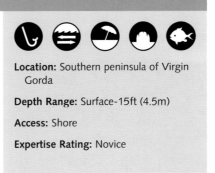

Location: Southern peninsula of Virgin Gorda

Depth Range: Surface-15ft (4.5m)

Access: Shore

Expertise Rating: Novice

You can access The Baths on your own by boat or by car. Daily ferries travel between Road Town (Tortola) and Spanish Town (Virgin Gorda), which is the closest ferry port to The Baths. You can also come as part of an organized daysail. Dive operators rarely stop here—if they do, it is during a surface interval.

The Baths can get somewhat overcrowded at times, especially in the wintertime high season. To avoid peak times, come early in the morning or late in the afternoon. A proposal to charge park entrance fees for The Baths and other national park areas is under consideration by the BVI government. The measure, which has many critics and supporters, would use the funds to develop facilities that accommodate the crowds.

Beautiful, clear waters make The Baths one of the BVI's premier attractions.

59 | Mountain Point

Mountain Point is a favorite with Virgin Gorda dive operators, mainly because of its proximity to their dive bases. The site is also a convenient stop on the way to popular Dog Islands sites.

Mountain Point is Virgin Gorda's westernmost peninsula. This site is exposed, and the tip of the point breaks, so the best diving usually takes place in the more protected areas south and west of the peninsula. The peninsula's north side features a fabulous cave, which is dive-

Location: 3 miles (5km) outside entrance to lagoon, northwest side of reef

Depth Range: 5-22m (16-72ft)

Access: Boat

Expertise Rating: Intermediate

able only when the north swells are not running.

Overhangs, sandy patches and coral heads host a variety of fish species. Parrotfish abound. When silversides are present (most common in the summer), tarpon feast. The site has a few caves and grottos, all of which have large, open entrances but are exposed to surge and swells from the north. Be particularly careful when exploring this area during the winter months, as swells can hit the peninsula hard.

Mountain Point is also a good place to spot lobsters, including the uncommon slipper lobster, known locally as a Spanish lobster. This critter looks especially prehistoric, with a shell protecting the creature from head to tail. Without the antennae or exposed legs common to other lobsters, it can be difficult to tell which end is which. Look but don't take—lobstering is strictly prohibited.

A dive light reflects on schooling fish.

60 The Invisibles

Because of constant trade winds and exposure to east and north swells, the north side of Virgin Gorda has very few sites that are diveable year-round. The Invisibles—on Eustatia Reef—is the only easily accessible site north of the Gorda Sound, and even it is both difficult to find and completely exposed to the elements.

Dive operators look for the breaking waves in rough seas to pinpoint this site's twin-rock formation. It is precisely the site's exposure that makes it worth visiting, even if you have to rough it a bit. Like many other offshore rocks around the BVI, the pinnacles' small crevices hide a large selection of tropical fish, and the occasional pelagic makes an appearance. The rocks are surrounded by gentle

Location: East of Necker Island

Depth Range: 15-65ft (4.6-20m)

Access: Boat

Expertise Rating: Intermediate

slopes that drop to a sandy bottom at about 65ft.

The site's highlights are the larger fish that come in from the open water, particularly from Horseshoe Reef. The reef, among the world's largest, begins to unravel just north of The Invisibles dive site. Permit, larger crevalle jacks, greater amberjacks and Atlantic spadefish are all good candidates at The Invisibles.

Anegada Dive Sites

About 15 miles (24km) north of Virgin Gorda lies the BVI's only completely coral island. One of the territory's most unique destinations, this low-lying sandy island offers 24 miles (39km) of pristine, mostly unpopulated coastline.

Extending southeast from Anegada's southern tip is a large coral reef shaped vaguely like a horseshoe. Horeshoe Reef is the world's third-largest continuous coral reef. Locally, it is considered one of the region's most treacherous cruising grounds, having claimed more than 350 vessels over the centuries of ship travel. With a few exceptions, these wrecks have been reduced to unrecognizable rubble scattered over miles and miles of thick coral. Though countless sunken riches reputedly still lie in wait, many large treasure-seeking expeditions have come up empty-handed.

The best treasure you're likely to find here is the island's unique wildlife. Anegada's fauna includes pink flamingos, the endemic Anegada iguana and countless migrating birds that inhabit the shallow salt flats and mangrove-fringed coastline. From February to April, humpback whales migrate to shallow waters west of the island to calf their young. In August, nurse and lemon sharks congregate around the shallow reefs north of the island to mate in large numbers.

Thousands of coral heads—many of them just under the water's surface—make up Horseshoe Reef.

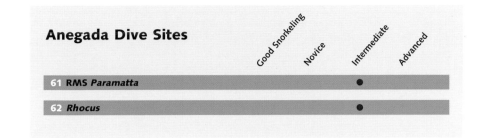

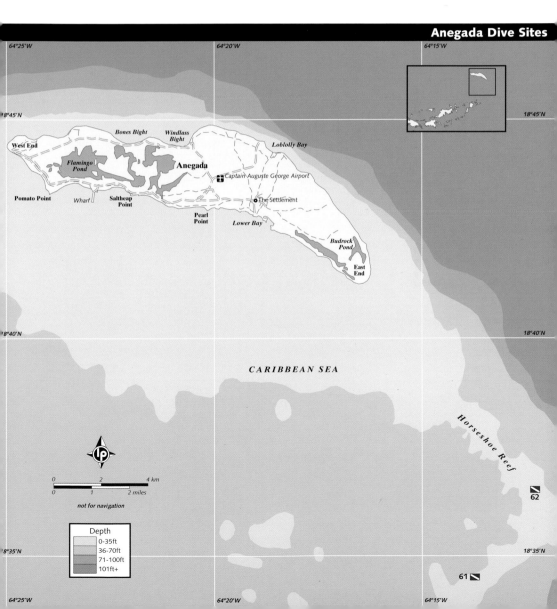

The diverse marine life and a pair of diveable wrecks should make Anegada an enticing—if isolated—destination for dive operators based on Virgin Gorda. In 1995, however, the government placed a moratorium on the reef, prohibiting anchoring in shallow waters. The ban was an attempt to curb illegal fishing in the area, which was decimating the marine life. Although diving is not illegal, the moratorium has made dive trips to this area significantly more difficult to arrange. Most operators do not visit Horseshoe Reef regularly, if at all. Some live-aboard vessels—the *Cuan Law*, most prominently—stay overnight in designated anchorages outside the banned area and offer regular diving on the reef.

Operators offer daytrips to the island (but not the reef) and snorkeling excursions to the north coast. Contact Killbride's Sunchaser Scuba or Dive BVI—both based on Virgin Gorda—for weekly trip schedules.

61 | RMS *Paramatta*

The 330ft *Paramatta*, a late-19th-century steel paddlewheel steamer, lies on the Atlantic (east) side of Horseshoe Reef. Like the *Rhone*, the *Paramatta* was part of the Royal Mail Steam Packet Company fleet, which delivered mail, passengers and cargo between Britain and the New World. In 1859 the vessel ran aground on

Location: East side of Horseshoe Reef

Depth Range: 10-40ft (3-12m)

Access: Live-aboard

Expertise Rating: Intermediate

More than 350 ships have perished in the shallow waters around Anegada Island.

the thick coral reef but did not sink immediately. A month's worth of desperate attempts to salvage her failed, ending in the abandonment of the vessel.

Exposed to wind and weather for much of the year, the wreck is seldom dived. She lies in very shallow water and can only be visited on days that are extremely calm. Large schools of fish inhabit her remains. Though the vessel has been largely leveled over the years, the *Paramatta* is worth visiting to see a piece of history—she is perhaps the only paddlewheel wreck in the Virgin Islands and was claimed by one of the area's most treacherous and historically feared reefs.

Migrating birds pass over Anegada's shallow coastal waters.

62 *Rhocus*

The *Rhocus*, a 380ft steel Greek freighter, sank on Anegada's Horseshoe Reef in 1929 after failing to clear the reef's southern corner. She was loaded with unusual cargo—a mass of cattle bones destined to become fertilizer. The bones still litter the wreck's cargo hold and the shallow waters surrounding it, giving the site a macabre appearance.

Although the wreck is mostly broken up, parts of the vessel—including the boilers, some winches, the anchor and its long heavy chain—are still visible. Many

Location: West of the southern tip of Horseshoe Reef

Depth Range: 5-40ft (1.5-12m)

Access: Live-aboard

Expertise Rating: Intermediate

fish have taken up permanent residency here. The *Rhocus* is a seldom-dived site, visited by only a few live-aboards.

Marine Life

Because the BVI offers so many different types of diving environments—from shallow coral gardens to a variety of geological formations to dramatic open-water wreck sites—divers will encounter an incredible diversity of marine life. There are about 60 hard and soft corals species and more than 178 different fish species in these waters. Rays sightings are common, with the seldom-seen manta ray making an occasional appearance. February to April, you may see, or more likely hear, humpback whales. Dolphins are commonly seen. You may encounter sharks, both the reef type and pelagics. In recent years there have been a number of whale-shark sightings, but they are still extremely rare. The following photo gallery is a sampling of the marine life you may encounter in the BVI.

Common names are used freely but are notoriously inaccurate and inconsistent. The two-part scientific name, usually shown in italics, is more precise. It consists of a genus name followed by a species name. A genus is a group of closely related species that share common features. A species is a recognizable group within a genus whose members are capable of interbreeding. Where the species or genus is unknown, the naming reverts to the next known level: family (F), order (O), class (C) or phylum (Ph).

Common Vertebrates

French angelfish
Pomacanthus paru

fairy basslet
Gramma loreto

saddled blenny
Malacoctenus triangulatus

sailfin blenny
Emblemaria pandionis

bridled burrfish
Chilomycterus antennatus

bigtooth cardinalfish
Apogon affinis

blue chromis
Chromis cyanea

coney (golden phase)
Epinephelus fulvus

spotted drum
Equetus punctatus

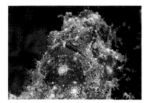

longlure frogfish
Antennarius multiocellatus

yellow goatfish
Mulloidichthys martinicus

graysby
Epinephelus cruentatus

smallmouth grunt
Haemulon chrysargreum

flying gurnard
Dactylopterus volitans

yellowhead jawfish
Opistognathus aurifrons

bar jack
Caranx ruber

bluestriped lizardfish
Synodus saurus

stoplight parrotfish
Sparisoma viride

sharpnose puffer
Canthigaster rostrata

Atlantic spadefish
Chaetodipterus faber

longspine squirrelfish
Holocentrus rufus

glassy sweeper
Pempheris schomburgki

blue tang
Acanthurus coeruleus

queen triggerfish
Balistes vetula

Common Invertebrates

channel clinging crab
Mitrax spinossimus

yellowline arrow crab
Stenorhynchus seticornis

elkhorn coral
Acropora palmata

pillar coral
Dendrogyra cylindrus

staghorn coral
Acropora cervicornis

rough fileclam
Lima scabra

Caribbean spiny lobster
Panulirus argus

Caribbean reef octopus
Octopus briareus

giant barrel sponge
Xestospongia muta

yellow tube sponge
Aplysina fistularis

Caribbean reef squid
Sepioteuthis sepioidea

Christmas tree worm
Spirobranchus giganteus

Hazardous Marine Life

Marine animals almost never attack divers, but many have defensive and offensive weaponry that can be triggered if they feel threatened or annoyed. The ability to recognize hazardous creatures is a valuable asset in avoiding accident and injury. The following are some of the potentially hazardous creatures most commonly found in the BVI.

Barracuda

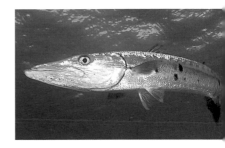

Barracuda are identifiable by their long, silver, cylindrical bodies and razorlike teeth protruding from an underslung jaw. They swim alone or in small groups, continually opening and closing their mouths, an action that looks daunting but actually assists their respiration. Though barracuda will hover near divers to observe, they are really somewhat shy, though they may be attracted by shiny objects that resemble fishing lures. Irrigate a barracuda bite with fresh water and treat with antiseptics, anti-tetanus and antibiotics.

Box Jellyfish (Sea Wasp)

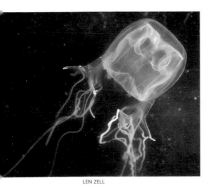

LEN ZELL

Box jellyfish, also known as sea wasps, are sometimes present in BVI waters. These are small, potent jellyfish with four stinging tentacles. Distinguished by their rectangular-shaped dome, with their long tentacles dangling from each of the four corners, box jellies generally swim just below the surface at night. The sting is very painful, and their venom is some of the most toxic of any marine animal, though most victims survive. Stay out of the water if box jellies are present. Treat immediately with a decontaminant such as vinegar, rubbing alcohol, baking soda, papain or dilute household ammonia.

Bristle Worm

Also called fire worms, bristle worms can be found all around the BVI in areas of coral rubble and seagrass beds. They have segmented bodies covered with either tufts or bundles of sensory hairs that extend in tiny, sharp, detachable bristles. If you touch one, the tiny stinging bristles lodge in your skin and cause a burning sensation that may be followed by a red spot or welt. Remove embedded bristles with adhesive tape, rubber cement or a commercial facial peel. Apply a decontaminant such as vinegar, rubbing alcohol or dilute ammonia.

Fire Coral

Although often mistaken for stony coral, fire coral is a hydroid colony that secretes a hard, calcareous skeleton. Fire coral grows in many different shapes, often encrusting or taking the form of a variety of reef structures. It is usually identifiable by its tan, mustard or brown color and fingerlike columns with whitish tips. The entire colony is covered by tiny pores and fine, hairlike projections nearly invisible to the unaided eye. Fire coral "stings" by discharging small, specialized cells called nematocysts. Contact causes a burning sensation that lasts for several minutes and may produce red welts on the skin. Do not rub the area, as you will only spread the stinging particles. Cortisone cream can reduce the inflammation, and antihistamine cream is good for killing the pain. Serious stings should be treated by a doctor.

Moray Eel

Distinguished by their long, thick, snakelike bodies and tapered heads, moray eels come in a variety of colors and patterns. Don't feed them or put your hand in a dark hole—eels have the unfortunate combination of sharp teeth and poor eyesight, and will bite if they feel threatened. If you are bitten, don't try to pull your hand away suddenly—the teeth slant backward and are extraordinarily sharp. Let the eel release it and then surface slowly. Treat with antiseptics, anti-tetanus and antibiotics.

Sea Urchin

Sea urchins tend to live in shallow areas near shore and come out of their shelters at night. They vary in coloration and size, with spines ranging from short and blunt to long and needle-sharp. The spines are the urchin's most dangerous weapon, easily able to penetrate neoprene wetsuits, booties and gloves. Treat minor punctures by extracting the spines and immersing the area in nonscalding hot water. More serious injuries require medical attention.

Scorpionfish

Scorpionfish are well-camouflaged creatures that have poisonous spines along their dorsal fins. They are often difficult to spot since they typically rest quietly on the bottom or on coral, looking more like rocks than fish. Practice good buoyancy control, and watch where you put your hands. Scorpionfish wounds can be excruciating. To treat a puncture, wash the wound and immerse it in nonscalding hot water for 30 to 90 minutes.

Shark

Sharks come in many shapes and sizes. They are most recognizable by their triangular dorsal fin. Though many species are shy, there are occasional attacks. About 25 species worldwide are considered dangerous to

STEVE ROSENBERG

humans. Sharks will generally not attack unless provoked, so don't taunt, tease or feed them. Avoid spearfishing, carrying fish baits or mimicking a wounded fish, and your likelihood of being attacked will greatly diminish. Face and quietly watch any shark that is acting aggressively and be prepared to push it away with a camera, knife or tank. If someone is bitten by a shark, stop the bleeding, reassure the patient, treat for shock and seek immediate medical aid.

Stingray

Identified by its diamond-shaped body and wide "wings," the stingray has one or two venomous spines at the base of its tail. Stingrays like shallow waters and tend to rest on silty or sandy bottoms, often burying themselves in the sand.

Often only the eyes, gill slits and tail are visible. These creatures are harmless unless you sit or step on them. Though injuries are uncommon, wounds are always extremely painful, and often deep and infective. Immerse wound in nonscalding hot water and seek medical aid.

Diving Conservation & Awareness

Threats to the BVI's marine environment include over-fishing, destruction of the fragile mangrove belt, and land erosion, which can suffocate near-shore coral reefs. The National Parks Trust (NPT) is a governmental agency that was established to manage the territory's national park lands both above and below the water. In addition to maintaining park facilities, the NPT strives to preserve park areas and protect endangered species, including marine turtles and the endemic Anegada iguana.

One of the most successful marine programs managed by the NPT is the dive-mooring system. Created by the BVI Dive Operators Association, the system was later adopted and continues to be maintained by the NPT. The mooring system has received international recognition as one of the best-implemented in the world.

The moorings use the Halas Method, a simple but sophisticated technique that protects the coral bottom from anchor damage as well as from chafing by the mooring itself. How is a mooring installed? First, a hole is drilled into the seafloor. Then a stainless-steel eye is cemented into the hole. Finally, a line with a pennant or painter at the end is attached to the eye—this is the part that you attach to your boat.

You must have an NPT permit to use the moorings. Permit fees go toward mooring maintenance and installation. Permits are available for a nominal fee from charter companies and some dive shops. The maximum vessel length is 50ft (15m). No overnighting is allowed, and anchoring inside national park boundaries is prohibited.

Mooring-System Markings

The NPT mooring system consists of more than 180 permanent moorings installed at all major dive and snorkel sites, as well as at some of the territory's other popular anchorages. The color of the mooring indicates the type of vessel that may use the mooring.

Orange or **red** moorings are for general day use.

Yellow moorings are for commercial dive boats only.

White moorings are for recreational or commercial vessels while diving only. There is a 90-minute time limit, and you must move on after you finish your dive to allow others to use the site.

Blue moorings are for dinghies and are found at snorkeling sites. Pull up and tie to the line itself.

Do not tie up too tightly—be sure to allow some slack on the mooring line. Also, it's better not to anchor between moored boats, as your vessel may swing and cause damage.

In addition to the NPT moorings, there are about 260 other permanent overnight moorings at popular anchorages throughout the BVI. You must pay a nightly fee to use these private moorings—someone from a nearby restaurant or bar usually collects the money. Day use is free.

It is illegal to remove any flora and fauna from BVI waters. Lobstering and the collection of conch, fish or corals of any kind are prohibited.

Responsible Diving

Dive sites tend to be located where the reefs and walls display the most beautiful corals and sponges. It only takes a moment—an inadvertently placed hand or knee, or a careless brush or kick with a fin—to destroy this fragile, living part of our delicate ecosystem. By following certain basic guidelines while diving, you can help preserve the ecology and beauty of the reefs:

1. Never drop boat anchors onto a coral reef and take care not to ground boats on coral. Encourage dive operators and regulatory bodies in their efforts to establish permanent moorings at appropriate dive sites.

2. Practice and maintain proper buoyancy control and avoid over-weighting. Be aware that buoyancy can change over the period of an extended trip. Initially you may breathe harder and need more weighting; a few days later you may breathe more easily and need less weight. Tip: Use your weight belt and tank position to maintain a horizontal position—raise them to elevate your feet, lower

The object of local protection efforts, the endemic Anegada iguana is found only in the BVI.

them to elevate your upper body. Also be careful about buoyancy loss: as you go deeper, your wetsuit compresses, as does the air in your BC.

3. Avoid touching living marine organisms with your body and equipment. Polyps can be damaged by even the gentlest contact. Never stand on or touch living coral. The use of gloves is no longer recommended: gloves make it too easy to hold on to the reef. The abrasion caused by gloves may be even more damaging to the reef than your hands are. If you must hold on to the reef, touch only exposed rock or dead coral.

4. Take great care in underwater caves. Spend as little time within them as possible, as your air bubbles can damage fragile organisms. Divers should take turns inspecting the interiors of small caves or under ledges to lessen the chances of damaging contact.

5. Be conscious of your fins. Even without contact, the surge from heavy fin strokes near the reef can do damage. Avoid full-leg kicks when diving close to the bottom and when leaving a photo scene. When you inadvertently kick something, stop kicking! It seems obvious, but some divers either panic or are totally oblivious when they bump something. When treading water in shallow reef areas, take care not to kick up clouds of sand. Settling sand can smother the delicate reef organisms.

6. Secure gauges, computer consoles and the octopus regulator so they're not dangling—they are like miniature wrecking balls to a reef.

Marine Conservation Organizations

Coral reefs and oceans are facing unprecedented environmental pressures. The following groups are actively involved in promoting responsible diving practices, publicizing environmental marine threats and lobbying for better policies.

Local Organizations

ARK (Association of Reef Keepers)
☎ 496-5526
ark@surfbvi.com

National Parks Trust
☎ 494-2069

International Organizations

CORAL: The Coral Reef Alliance
☎ 510-848-0110
www.coral.org

Ocean Futures
☎ 805-899-8899
www.oceanfutures.com

Cousteau Society
☎ 757-523-9335
www.cousteausociety.org

ReefKeeper International
☎ 305-358-4600
www.reefkeeper.org

Project AWARE Foundation
☎ 714-540-0251
www.projectaware.org

7. When swimming in strong currents, be extra careful about leg kicks and handholds.

8. Photographers should take extra precautions as cameras and equipment affect buoyancy. Changing f-stops, framing a subject and maintaining position for a photo often conspire to prohibit the ideal "no-touch" approach on a reef. When you must use "holdfasts," choose them intelligently (i.e., use one finger only for leverage off an area of dead coral).

9. Resist the temptation to collect or buy coral or shells. Aside from the ecological damage, taking home marine souvenirs depletes the beauty of a site and spoils other divers' enjoyment.

10. Ensure that you take home all your trash and any litter you may find as well. Plastics in particular pose a serious threat to marine life.

11. Resist the temptation to feed fish. You may disturb their normal eating habits, encourage aggressive behavior or feed them food that is detrimental to their health.

12. Minimize your disturbance of marine animals. Don't ride on the backs of turtles or manta rays as this can cause them great anxiety.

A group of divers learns underwater fish-survey techniques.

Listings

Telephone Calls

The BVI has excellent (though extremely expensive) communications services, including standard land lines, marine cellular communications and plenty of Internet access and email services. To call the BVI from the U.S., Canada or another part of the Caribbean, dial 1 + 284 + the local seven-digit number. From elsewhere, dial your country's international access code + 284 + the local number.

Accommodations

Accommodations in the BVI range from campgrounds to exclusive 5-star resorts. Some hotels cater specifically to the diving crowd with services such as wet lockers or drying areas for diving gear. That said, many diving operators will care for your gear overnight, eliminating the need for diver-oriented lodging. A marine alternative to traditional lodging options is to charter a bareboat or crewed yacht. See Yacht Charters for more information.

The following is a partial listing of BVI accommodations convenient to diving areas. A complete list of hotels, inns, guesthouses, villas and apartments is available from the tourist office or from the BVI *Welcome Magazine* and its online counterpart at www.bviwelcome.com.

Tortola

Brewers Bay Campground
(30+ tents & bare sites)
Brewers Bay
☎ 494-3463
Showers, toilets, restaurant, bar

Heritage Villas
(9 villas)
Windy Hill, above Carrot Bay
☎ 494-5842 fax: 495-4100
www.go-bvi.com/heritage villas
heritage@candwbvi.net
Pool, restaurant, kitchens

Ole Works Inn & Quito's Gazebo
(18 rooms)
Cane Garden Bay
☎ 495-4837 fax: 495-9618
www.bviguide.com/ole.html
oleworks@candwbvi.net
Live entertainment, restaurant

Long Bay Beach Resort & Villas
(72 rooms, 21 villas)
Long Bay
☎ 495-4252 fax: 495-4677
toll-free ☎ 800-729-9599 (U.S.)
www.longbay.com
info@longbay.com
Pools, watersports, tennis, restaurants, bars, spa, gym

The Moorings – Mariner Inn
(40 rooms)
Road Town
☎ 494-2332 fax: 494-2226
toll-free ☎ 800-535-7289
www.moorings.com
yacht@moorings.com
Yacht charters, pool, dive shop, watersports, restaurant

Nanny Cay Resort & Marina
(40 rooms)
Nanny Cay
☎ 494-4895 fax: 494-0555
toll-free ☎ 800-742-4276 (U.S.)
nannycay@surfbvi.com
Pool, dive shop, watersports, tennis, bicycles,
restaurants

Prospect Reef Resort
(137 rooms)
Road Town
☎ 494-3311 fax: 494-5595
toll-free ☎ 800-356-8937 (U.S. and Canada)
www.prospectreef.com
inquiries@prospectreef.com
Pools, dive shop, watersports, restaurants,
gym

Sebastian's on the Beach
(26 rooms, 9 villas)
Little Apple Bay
☎ 495-4212 fax: 495-4466
toll-free ☎ 800-336-4870 (U.S.)
www.sebastiansbvi.com
info@sebastiansbvi.com
Restaurant

The Sugar Mill
(24 rooms)
Apple Bay
☎ 495-4355 fax: 495-4696
toll-free ☎ 800-462-8834 (U.S.),
800-209-6874 (Canada)
www.sugarmillhotel.com
sugmill@surfbvi.com
Pool, restaurant, no children allowed
December to April

Jost Van Dyke

White Bay Campground
(cabins & bare sites)
Jost Van Dyke

☎ 495-9358 or 495-9312
Showers, toilets, guest kitchen, restaurant,
bar

Virgin Gorda

Biras Creek Resort
(33 rooms)
North Sound
☎ 494-3555 fax: 494-3557
www.biras.com
biras@biras.com
Pool, watersports, tennis, bicycles,
restaurant, bar

Bitter End Yacht Club
(85 rooms)
North Sound
☎ 494-2746 fax: 494-4756
toll-free ☎ 800-872-2392
www.beyc.com
binfo@beyc.com
Live-aboard boats, pool, watersports,
restaurants, bars

Leverick Bay Resort & Marina
(16 rooms)
Leverick Bay
☎ 495-7421 fax: 495-7367
toll-free ☎ 800-848-7081 (U.S.),
800-463-9396 (Canada)
www.leverickbay.com
leverick@surfbvi.com
Pool, dive shop, watersports, tennis,
restaurant, bar

Little Dix Bay Resort
(98 rooms)
Little Dix Bay
☎ 495-5555 fax: 495-5661
toll-free ☎ 800-928-3000
www.littledixbay.com
ldbhotel@caribsurf.com
Watersports, tennis, restaurants, bar

Peter Island

Peter Island Resort
(52 rooms, 3 villas)
Peter Island
☎ 495-2000 fax: 495-2500
toll-free ☎ 800-542-4624 (U.S.)

www.peterisland.com
reservations@peterisland.com
Pool, watersports, tennis, bicycles, restaurants, bars, dive shop, gym, spa

Cooper Island

Cooper Island Beach Club
(12 rooms)
Cooper Island
☎ 495-9084 fax: 495-9180

toll-free ☎ 800-542-4624 (U.S.)
www.cooper-island.com
info@cooper-island.com
Dive shop, restaurant, bar

Anegada

Anegada Reef Hotel
(16 rooms)
Setting Point
☎ 495-8002 fax: 495-9362
www.anegadareef.com
info@anegadareef.com
Watersports, restaurant, bar

Neptune's Campground
(bare sites)
Anegada
☎ 495-9439
Showers, toilets, beds, restaurant

Diving Services

Aquaventure Scuba Services
Inner Harbour Marina, Tortola
☎ 494-4320 fax: 494-5608
www.aquaventurebvi.com
aquavent@surfbvi.com
Sales: yes **Rentals:** yes
Boat: 35ft (10 divers)
Classes: PADI & NAUI Open Water to Divemaster

Baskin in the Sun
Prospect Reef Resort & Soper's Hole Marina (Tortola); Peter Island
☎ 494-2858 fax: 494-4304
toll-free ☎ 800-650-2084 (U.S.)
www.dive-baskin.com
reservations@baskininthesun.com
Sales: yes **Rentals:** yes
Boats: 42ft (30 divers), 34ft (15 divers), 32ft (10 divers)
Classes: PADI, NAUI & SSI Open Water to Instructor

Blue Water Divers
Nanny Cay Marina, Tortola
☎ 494-2847 fax: 494-0198
Hodge's Creek Marina, Tortola
☎ 495-1200 fax:495-1210
www.ultimatebvi.com/bluewater/index.html
bwdbvi@surfbvi.com
Sales: yes **Rentals:** yes
Boats: 45ft (20 divers), 39ft (15 divers), 34ft (10 divers), 32ft (6 divers)
Classes: PADI Open Water to Divemaster

Dive BVI
Virgin Gorda Yacht Harbour, Leverick Bay & Marina Cay

☎ 495-5513 fax: 494-5347
toll-free ☎ 800-848-7078 (U.S.)
www.divebvi.com
info@divebvi.com
Sales: yes **Rentals:** yes
Boats: 45ft (16 divers), 38ft (14 divers), 35ft (10 divers), 28ft (8 divers)
Classes: PADI Open Water to Divemaster

Killbride's Sunchaser Scuba
Bitter End Yacht Club, Virgin Gorda
☎ 495-9638 fax: 495-7549
toll-free ☎ 800-932-4286 (U.S.)
www.come.to/bvi
sunscuba@surfbvi.com
Sales: no **Rentals:** yes
Boats: 42ft (20 divers), 38ft (10 divers)
Classes: PADI Open Water to Divemaster

Sail Caribbean
Hodge's Creek Marina, Tortola
☎ 495-1675 fax: 631-754-3362
www.sailcaribbean.com
info@sailcaribbean.com
Sales: no **Rentals:** no
Boats: 36ft (18 divers), 25ft (8 divers)
Classes: PADI Open Water to Divemaster

UBS Dive Center
Harbour View Marina, Tortola
☎ 494-0024 fax: 494-0623 cell: 496-8475
www.scubabvi.com
mail@scubabvi.com
Sales: yes **Rentals:** yes
Boats: 25ft (6 divers), 20ft (4 divers)
Classes: PADI Open Water to Divemaster

Underwater Safaris
The Moorings (Tortola) & Cooper Island
☎ 494-3235 fax: 494-5322
toll-free ☎ 800-537-7032 (U.S.)
www.underwatersafaris.com

info@underwatersafaris.com
Sales: yes **Rentals:** yes
Boats: 30ft (12 divers), 30ft (12 divers), 42ft
(21 divers)
Classes: PADI Open Water to Divemaster

Live-Aboards

SV *Cuan Law*
Trimarine Boat Company
☎ 494-2490 fax: 494-5774
toll-free ☎ 800-648-3393 (U.S.)
www.bvidiving.com
cuanlaw@surfbvi.com
Home Port: Road Town, Tortola
Description: 105ft (32m) aluminum catamaran (20 passengers)
Duration: 6 nights (diving & shore excursions)
Other: all-inclusive, watersports, A/C, E6
photo processing, video editing

SV *Promenade*
Promenade Cruises
☎/fax: 496-0999
toll-free ☎ 800-526-5503 (U.S.)
www.yachtpromenade.com
saildive@yachtpromenade.com
Home Port: Road Town, Tortola
Description: 65ft (20m) fiberglass catamaran
(10 passengers)
Duration: 6 or 7 nights (diving & shore
excursions)
Other: all-inclusive, watersports, A/C

SV *Serendipity*
Serendipity Adventures Ltd.
☎ 495-2612 boat: 496-7557
www.sailserendipity.com
ecosail@surfbvi.com
Home Port: Beef Island, Tortola
Description: 50ft (15m) fiberglass monohull
(6 passengers)
Duration: 7 nights (snorkeling & shore
excursions)
Other: all-inclusive, eco-oriented snorkeling
& shore excursions, divers must bring own
equipment

SV *Wanderlust*
Wanderlust Yacht Vacations
☎ 494-2405 boat: 496-8449
toll free ☎ 800-724-5284 (U.S.)
www.wanderlustcharters.com
wanderer@surfbvi.net
Home Port: Beef Island, Tortola
Description: 65ft (20m) fiberglass trimaran
(12 passengers)
Duration: 7 nights (diving & shore excursions)
Other: all-inclusive, watersports, A/C

Yacht Charters

The BVI is one of the world's most popular yachting destinations. Charters are available crewed or bareboat (without crew). Bareboat yachts are available with sail or with power engine. Vessels vary in size and comfort and can accommodate as few as two and as many as 18 people. The following is a partial list of the best-known charter companies in the BVI. Any number of privately owned yachts are also available in a range of sizes and prices—one of the BVI's many yacht brokers can help you make arrangements.

**Cane Garden Bay Pleasure Boat &
Watersports**
Cane Garden Bay, Tortola
☎ 495-9660
Services: bareboat (power) day charters

Catamaran Charters
Nanny Cay Marina, Tortola
☎ 494-6661 fax: 494-6698
toll-free ☎ 800-262-0308 (U.S.)
Services: bareboat (sail) and crewed (sail);
optional provisioning

Endless Summer II
Nanny Cay Marina, Tortola
☎ 494-3656
toll-free ☎ 800-368-9905 (U.S.)
www.endlesssummer.com
info@endlesssummer.com
Services: crewed (sail); provisioned

Horizon Yacht Charters
Nanny Cay Marina, Tortola
☎ 494-8787 fax: 494-8989
toll free ☎ 877-494-8787 (U.S.)
www.horizonyachtcharters.com
info@horizonyachtcharters.com
Services: bareboat (sail) and crewed (sail);
optional provisioning

King Charters Ltd.
Nanny Cay Marina, Tortola
☎ 494-5820 fax: 494-5821
www.kingcharters.com
king@surfbvi.com
Services: bareboat (power) and crewed
(power) day charters; optional provisioning

The Moorings
Road Town, Tortola
☎ 494-2331 fax: 494-2226
toll-free ☎ 800-535-7289 (U.S.)

www.moorings.com
yacht@moorings.com
Services: bareboat (sail) and crewed (sail);
optional provisioning

Sunsail
Soper's Hole Marina, Tortola
☎ 495-4740 fax: 495-4301
www.sunsail.com
sstortola@candwbvi.net
Services: bareboat (sail) and crewed (sail);
optional provisioning

Virgin Traders
Nanny Cay Marina, Tortola
☎ 495-2526 fax: 495-2678
toll-free ☎ 888-684-6486
cruising@virgin-traders.com
Services: bareboat (power) and crewed
(power); optional provisioning

Voyage Charters
Soper's Hole Marina, Tortola
☎ 494-0740 fax: 494-0741
toll-free ☎ 888-869-2436 (U.S.)
www.voyagecharters.com
info@voyagecharters.com
Services: bareboat (sail) and crewed (sail);
optional provisioning

Underwater Photo & Video Services

Mauricio Handler Photography
Tortola
☎/fax: 494-0340
www.handlerphoto.com
mauricio@handlerphoto.com
Commercial photo services, week-long
underwater photo workshops, general
camera advice, Aquatica professional camera
systems dealer

Rainbow Visions
Prospect Reef Marina, Tortola
☎ 494-2749 fax: 494-6390
www.rainbowvisions.com
rainbow@surfbvi.com
Professional underwater photo and video
services; underwater still- & video-camera
rentals & sales, including tapes (including
Mini-DV), batteries and refrigerated film;
E6 processing for 35mm and 120/220 film;
video editing & PAL/NTSC video transfers

Tourist Office

British Virgin Islands Tourist Board
AKARA Building, Road Town, Tortola
☎ 494-3134 fax: 494-3866
toll-free ☎ 800-835-8530 (U.S.)
bvitourb@surfbvi.com

Index

dive sites covered in this book appear in **bold** type

Lonely Planet Pisces Books

The **Diving & Snorkeling** guides cover top destinations worldwide. Beautifully illustrated with full-color photos throughout, the series explores the best diving and snorkeling areas and prepares divers for what to expect when they get there. Each site is described in detail, with information on suggested ability levels, depth, visibility and, of course, marine life. There's basic topside information as well for each destination.

Also check out dive guides to:

Australia's
Great Barrier Reef

Australia: Southeast Coast

Bahamas: Family Islands
& Grand Bahama

Bahamas: Nassau
& New Providence

Bali & Lombok

Bermuda

Bonaire

Cocos Island

Curaçao

Florida Keys

Guam & Yap

Jamaica

Monterey Peninsula &
Northern California

Pacific Northwest

Papua New Guinea

Red Sea

Roatan & Honduras'
Bay Islands

Scotland

Seychelles

Southern California

Tahiti
& French Polynesia

Texas

Thailand

Turks & Caicos

Vanuatu